"Most parents don't realize that there is a science to raising happy, healthy, and successful children. Teachers spend years learning and developing their skills based on this knowledge, but it is rare for parents to benefit from all this expertise. Ms. Holewa and Ms. Rice have written a very practical book, which though easy to read, is clearly based on years of teaching and caring for children. Every parent will find some gem to help make their job a little easier and a lot more fun."

—Lawrence E. Shapiro, Ph.D., author of
The Secret Language of Children

Practical and Playful Ways to Help
Children Listen, Learn, and Cooperate at Home

WHAT KINDERGARTEN TEACHERS KNOW

Lisa Holewa and Joan Rice

A PERIGEE BOOK

A PERIGEE BOOK
Published by the Penguin Group
Penguin Group (USA) Inc.
375 Hudson Street, New York, New York 10014, USA

Penguin Group (Canada), 90 Eglinton Avenue East, Suite 700, Toronto, Ontario M4P 2Y3, Canada
(a division of Pearson Penguin Canada Inc.)
Penguin Books Ltd., 80 Strand, London WC2R 0RL, England
Penguin Group Ireland, 25 St. Stephen's Green, Dublin 2, Ireland (a division of Penguin Books Ltd.)
Penguin Group (Australia), 250 Camberwell Road, Camberwell, Victoria 3124, Australia
(a division of Pearson Australia Group Pty. Ltd.)
Penguin Books India Pvt. Ltd., 11 Community Centre, Panchsheel Park, New Delhi—110 017, India
Penguin Group (NZ), 67 Apollo Drive, Rosedale, North Shore 0632, New Zealand
(a division of Pearson New Zealand Ltd.)
Penguin Books (South Africa) (Pty.) Ltd., 24 Sturdee Avenue, Rosebank, Johannesburg 2196,
South Africa

Penguin Books Ltd., Registered Offices: 80 Strand, London WC2R 0RL, England

While the author has made every effort to provide accurate telephone numbers and Internet addresses at the time of publication, neither the publisher nor the author assumes any responsibility for errors, or for changes that occur after publication. Further, the publisher does not have any control over and does not assume any responsibility for author or third-party websites or their content.

Copyright © 2008 by Lisa Holewa and Joan Rice
Interior illustrations by Kim Abbati
Cover art by Ward Schumaker
Cover design by Petra Andersson-Pardini
Text design by Tiffany Estreicher

First edition: May 2008

Library of Congress Cataloging-in-Publication Data

Holewa, Lisa.
    What kindergarten teachers know : practical and playful ways for parents to help children listen, learn, and cooperate at home / Lisa Holewa and Joan Rice.— 1st ed.
      p. cm.
    ISBN 978-0-399-53424-9
    1. Child development.   2. Parent and child.   I. Rice, Joan.   II. Title.
    HQ767.9.H65 2008
    649'.124—dc22   2007048262

PRINTED IN THE UNITED STATES OF AMERICA

10 9 8 7 6 5 4 3 2 1

Most Perigee books are available at special quantity discounts for bulk purchases for sales promotions, premiums, fund-raising, or educational use. Special books, or book excerpts, can also be created to fit specific needs. For details, write: Special Markets, Penguin Group (USA) Inc., 375 Hudson Street, New York, New York 10014.

For great teachers everywhere,
For inspiring and teaching families
and changing the world bit by bit.

For our children, Hannah and Emily, and Maya, Jack, and Lucy,
For teaching us so much more than we ever hoped.

And for our husbands, Roy and John,
For learning and growing along with us.

—JR and LH

ACKNOWLEDGMENTS

We began this book sitting around kitchen tables and picnic tables one summer, Joan's older daughters watching Lisa's little ones while Joan patiently explained the childhood development theories behind her simple classroom tricks. This book may have remained an extended conversation in backyards and kitchens, if not for the help of:

- Our agent, Marilyn Allen, whom we met at a writing conference the following summer, who immediately understood and embraced the book's concept.
- Writing coach Scott Edelstein, whom we met at the same conference. He kept us on track when theory threatened to overwhelm tips with this advice: If Maria Montessori rang the doorbell as your three kids were screaming and dinner was burning, you wouldn't talk child development theory—you'd hand her a kid and ask for help. That became our goal: to grab a kid and offer practical, meaningful help.

- Christine DeSmet and her colleagues at the University of Wisconsin–Madison, who organized that conference—their work gives all writers a chance to be heard.

- And most importantly, our editor, Maria Gagliano, who believed in this book and us enough to gently yet persistently ask the tough questions that made the book much stronger.

We'd also like to acknowledge Lisa's old college roommate and her children's pediatrician, Dr. Jenny Thomas, who reviewed the material and provided practical guidance; writer Carolyn Alfvin, who read many drafts of the manuscript and gave helpful feedback; Joan's teaching colleagues, especially Annette Sabo and Nancy Meier, who shared ideas and suggestions; and Joan's niece Leah Andrysczyk, who is studying to be a teacher and whose fresh ideas and enthusiasm are inspiring.

CONTENTS

Foreword by Jacquelyn Mitchard   xiii
Introduction: What Kindergarten Teachers Know   xvii

1. SECRETS GOOD TEACHERS KNOW ABOUT YOUR CHILD   1
The Basics of Child Development • How Children Develop Socially
Between Three and Five • How an Understanding of How Children
Learn Guides Teachers

2. THE TEACHER SETS THE TONE   19
Why It's Important to Respect Who You Are • How Teachers Develop
a Teaching Philosophy • Creating Your Own Philosophy Statement

3. HELPING YOUR CHILD LISTEN AND FOLLOW DIRECTIONS   25
How Classroom Techniques Can Guide You • Handling
Transitions: The Key to Getting Through Your Day • Getting Your
Child's Attention • Giving Your Directions: Make Them Simple and
Fun • Transitions at Home: Getting Up, Getting Going, Getting
Settled • Handling Separation Anxiety

4. ORGANIZING YOUR HOME   63
How Classroom Organization Techniques Can Help at Home •
The Physical Space • The Items Within Each Room: Organizing Your
Stuff • Decorating: Adding the Personal Touches • The Teacher's Desk:
Why Some Areas Can Be Off-Limits

5. ORGANIZING YOUR DAYS 77

Helping Your Day Run Smoothly • How to Create a Workable Schedule • Developing Routines or Procedures • Using Calendars Effectively • Assigning Tasks or Household Jobs

6. MAKING AND USING RULES CREATIVELY 99

A Handful of Rules Can Do the Job • How Should Your Rules Be Formed? • When the Rules Are Broken: Balancing Love and Authority • To Reward or Not to Reward?

7. RESOLVING CONFLICTS AND RESPONDING TO STRONG EMOTIONS 121

How Your Child Can Learn These Skills • Learning to Recognize and Name Emotions • Understanding That Feelings Change • Understanding the Difference Between Feelings and Actions • Learning Self-Soothing, or Relaxation Techniques • Learning to Find Solutions

8. THE IMPORTANCE OF PLAY 153

Why and How You Should Play with Your Young Child Every Day • What Is "True Play" and Why Is It Important? • Influencing the Detail of Your Child's Play • Using Play to Guide Your Child Through Stress or Difficulties • Teaching Your Child How to Be a Friend and Make a Friend • Playing with Your Child Builds Trust and a Healthy Relationship

9. BUILDING FAMILY AND COMMUNITY 171

How Teachers Transform Their Classrooms • How Family Meals Can Build Community • Around the House • Anytime

10. WHERE TO GO FROM HERE: AS YOUR CHILD GROWS AND
  CHANGES   183

Adapting the Techniques You've Mastered • Off You Go

Teacher Biographies   189
Other Resources   193

FOREWORD

When it comes to hands-on, experience-based, commonsense, and compassionate advice about the real ways to raise well-adjusted and happy kids, Joan Rice and Lisa Holewa's book is among the few that truly delivers. To top it off, this book is fun and easy to reference and read.

To be honest, when Lisa and Joan gave me the manuscript for *What Kindergarten Teachers Know*, I thought, "This book sounds good and they are nice," so I was happy to skim it and give them some guidance. When they asked me to write a foreword for the book, I had to beg off. I was up to my knees in one novel, up to my ears in another. I was juggling so many pieces of journalism that I was sending completed stories to editors who hadn't commissioned them. I was getting two kids ready to return to elementary school, two to college, one to preschool. I was preparing to teach at a conference. I was trying to understand why my four-year-old had the personality of a hardened second-story man and, with one exception, all my children were resolute and unregenerate liars.

It was a busy Thursday morning when it struck me that I was... using the information I had learned in *Kindergarten Teachers* to work out issues with my obstreperous four-year-old and my shy yet adorably devious eight-year-old. I was using a book for which I had refused to write a foreword. I was looking things up in a *parenting* book—I! The über-mom. A mother since before I was born! A mother termed by one of her children a solid C+ mom with A's in my favorite subjects (Hey, thanks Marty!), sole support of a family that included a husband, seven kids (six still at home), a dog, two horses, and a field mouse. Writer of hundreds of articles on everything from sibling rivalry to teenage responsibility.

I had not only read Dr. Spock, I *knew* Dr. Spock.

I thought I was doing most things properly, and wondered why not all of them were working. In fact, my mischievous eleven-year-old daughter had given me a copy of *Nanny 911* for my birthday. That book, along with *Baby and Child Care* and *The Moral Life of Children*, had pages marked with metal tabs. The shelf of other books on parenting techniques given me during my years as a contributing editor for *Parenting* magazine and *Wondertime* were simply there for me to dust. That Thursday, when I found myself using the advice in *What Kindergarten Teachers Know*, I decided to pass those other books on to other parents.

But I won't be parting with *What Kindergarten Teachers Know* for quite some time.

It taught this old dog new tricks.

Whether you're a newbie or a veteran, a grandma or a childcare provider, it can teach you, too.

—Jacquelyn Mitchard,
author, *The Deep End of the Ocean*;
contributing editor, *Wondertime* magazine

INTRODUCTION

WHAT KINDERGARTEN TEACHERS KNOW

I stood in my oldest daughter's kindergarten classroom as she and twenty other five-year-olds hurried to line up by the door and wait for their teacher's instructions. Not all eyes were on Mrs. Rice—one boy was poking the girl in front of him, another struggled to tie his shoes, a girl lingered near the carpet squares. But it was just a few weeks ago that this was a jumbled hodgepodge of kids, each too busy doing their own thing to follow directions, put down their toys, or work together as a group.

Now, six weeks into the school year, they were a class. They stood in line, reasonably quiet, waiting to hear what came next, ready to do what the teacher asked. It was such a change from the chaotic early days of school, when I first was in the classroom, that I had to wonder: How had this transformation taken place?

I looked at Maya, my daughter, small but standing tall at the line's midpoint. "Go to your lockers. Put on your coats. Get your backpacks," Mrs. Rice told the students calmly. She held up three fingers.

"Locker," she said, touching one of her fingers. "Coat," she said and held the second. "Backpack," she said, gripping the third.

"Locker, coat, backpack," she repeated. "Locker, coat, backpack."

And off they went into the hallway, happily—like fun-loving children, not programmed robots—but with a job to do all the same.

Clearly there were secrets to be learned here.

Watching my daughter, I imagined how much easier life would be if I had this same child at home, one who followed my directions, rather than dawdling, postponing, and endlessly negotiating. I envisioned my home as cheerful, organized, and as easy to maintain as this kindergarten classroom. And I imagined having help getting things done around the house, rather than grumbling and doing everything myself.

I looked around the classroom, brightly decorated and clearly organized. The day's schedule was posted at the back, near the weather report. Sections of the room clearly were for play, art, classwork. Each child had a cubby for tools—crayons, markers, glue sticks. It would be easy, even for a stranger in this classroom, to put everything where it belonged.

But most importantly, there was Mrs. Rice, directing traffic and keeping the kids on track. Somehow, she managed to give the children the individual attention they needed—answering questions, listening to stories, offering praise—without letting the class as a whole fall into chaos.

How did she do it?

Standing in her classroom, watching Mrs. Rice with her students, I knew she was working a kind of magic. My question was: Could I work the same magic in my own home, with my children? Was there a way to learn these tricks—to understand the secrets behind the magic—and adapt them to work outside the classroom?

I realized, of course, that teachers have some advantages over parents. For starters, simply, they're not the child's parent. Children are naturally inclined to put their best and most obedient faces on for the outside world, saving much of their defiance, misbehavior, and meltdowns for the security of their own home. And there's the "peer pressure" element in the classroom, where a child who might otherwise argue about, say, waiting at the door will simply fall into line if that's what her classmates are doing. And of course, teachers have years of specialized training that goes far beyond what we parents learn in bits and pieces while on the job.

Still, I could see that plenty of Mrs. Rice's tricks could be easily mastered by parents.

One of the most striking examples for me that day was also among the simplest: When it was time for the children to stop their work and move on to a new activity, Mrs. Rice directed those who hadn't finished to put the work in their "Not Done" pouch, a file hanging at one end of the work area. And the children who normally might have argued or whined because they wanted to finish instead knew they would have time and opportunity to come back to this work later. This was brilliant to me, with a daughter who always wanted to finish her project when it was time to have lunch or run to the store or otherwise move on to something else. It suddenly struck me that what she needed was not a firmer instruction to stop, but an honest acknowledgment that she wasn't done and the knowledge that she'd be able to finish later. Surely I could do that at home.

Another marvel: When Mrs. Rice wanted to interrupt the children and have them listen to her instructions for what came next, she clapped: Clap clap (pause) clap. The children knew to clap back, repeating the pattern: Clap clap (pause) clap. Then she clapped again: Clap (pause) clap clap clap. And they repeated the sequence. At that point they were clearly paying attention and she gave her instructions. So there were alternatives to endlessly repeating my child's name, becoming louder and more insistent each time!

Seeing my daughter with her classmates, I wondered: What does a good early childhood teacher offer to her students? Why do they blossom under her instruction, becoming self-sufficient, proud of their skills, confident in their ability to accomplish and learn? What does she know that transforms an assortment of self-centered and demanding kids into classmates who can take turns, listen to each other, help with cleanup and organization, and stay on task?

I decided to learn the tricks that Mrs. Rice and other good early childhood teachers use in their classrooms and see if they could fit into the home environment. As a former reporter (I worked for ten years for the Associated Press), I already knew how to gather information. And with three young children, I certainly had a good sense of the questions I wanted to ask. I enlisted the help of Mrs. Rice, an intelligent, loving, and intuitive teacher with two daughters; a master's degree in early childhood education; and a "Teacher of the Year" award from our city's children's museum.

We spent many afternoons together, Mrs. Rice patiently explaining childhood development theory and how kids learn, until I could understand it clearly, ask meaningful questions, and see how it might apply at home. Although you'll hear mainly my voice throughout this book—the voice of a parent with young children learning how to translate classroom techniques to home—the content of the book comes from both of us.

The teachers we interviewed are some of this nation's best. We spoke with Patrice McCrary, whose many awards include being named 2003 Kentucky State Teacher of the Year—she greets each child at the door of her classroom every morning with a hug and some kind words. Disney Teacher Award honoree Pauline Jacroux told us about the everyday lessons her students learn in their lush garden outside their classroom in Hawaii. And 2007 Oregon State Teacher of the Year Jackie Cooke described the simple tags she attaches to small stuffed animals, giving her students hints on getting through stressful moments.

Clever early childhood teachers have so many wonderful tricks. Many require no special materials, no training, no preparation—just a sense of fun and a willingness to try something different. Two simple and fun examples are Elephant Ears and Marshmallow Feet. When you want your child to listen to an instruction, stop yourself from saying: "Listen to me." Instead, announce something like: "It's time to put on your elephant ears!" and hook your fingers over your ears so your hands cup behind them, like an elephant's ear. Show your child how to do the same thing. That simple act—the fun of doing something different, the actual physical action of carrying it through—will put your child in a "listening" frame of mind, so your next instructions will actually be heard. (As a variation, you could simply ask: "Do you have on your listening ears?" and gently touch your child's ears.) When you want your child to walk quietly down the hallway so as not to wake a napping sibling, or when you just want to get out to the car and she's being resistant, tell her to walk with "Marshmallow Feet." Magically, the simple act of walking carefully becomes fun and adventurous—a challenge.

We'll show you techniques like these that great teachers use every day in their classrooms—sometimes to avoid meltdown situations, other times to get the kids on track and listening, and sometimes to help the children manage their emotions. We'll explain why these teacher tricks work, and find ways you can adapt them to use at home. We'll help you understand how your child is growing, how you can help, and how to grow together as a family, in much the same way that a good early childhood teacher helps her students become a class.

Throughout the book, we've also included simple one-page activity sheets that are based on techniques great teachers use in the classroom. While we translated them for the home, they are based on the same principles and theories underlying great classroom techniques—grounded in widely accepted research and developmentally appropriate practices, such as those outlined by the National Association for the Education of Young Children (NAEYC) and the American Academy of Pediatrics.

These techniques can be used whether you have one preschool-aged child at home or three, or a preschool-age child with an older school-age sibling and a young toddler (or whatever other combination you can imagine). Where appropriate, we'll include a sentence or two adapting the technique for multiple children.

Although these techniques are geared toward children ages three to six, the things you'll learn will help your child for a lifetime: how children can learn to resolve their own conflicts, ways they can calm themselves, even what "true play" means and how it can strengthen and transform your relationship with your child.

But before we begin, I want to say that this book is not designed to teach you the "right" way to parent your child (or to convince you that everything you've done until now has been wrong). We're not giving you a step-by-step blueprint, promising it will build the perfect child. Most of all, we're not asking you to change who you are as a parent—but instead to trust yourself as a parent.

We're sharing tools to help you get through the most difficult parts of your days more easily. We're teaching you what great teachers know. And we're hoping these techniques, developed and tested in the nation's best early childhood classrooms, will help you parent with less frustration, more confidence, and perhaps a greater sense of joy.

—Lisa Holewa

1

SECRETS GOOD TEACHERS KNOW ABOUT YOUR CHILD

The Basics of Child Development

When I started learning the techniques good teachers use in their classrooms, my mission was straightforward: Find simple tricks and adapt them to make life easier at home. But the more I learned, the more I realized that the best tricks work because they are in tune with where children are developmentally. In other words, the techniques a good early childhood teacher uses in her classroom actually fit who the children are. The best ones help them grow in some important way.

For instance, I needed to spend only a few minutes in Mrs. Rice's classroom to hear her singing—singing cleanup songs, singing instructions, singing songs that praised the children. I thought it was a nice—and brave!—way to keep the mood positive and cheerful. And it was. But the rhymes she makes up as she sings are also important for a less obvious reason. The rhyming words actually help her students master prereading skills. I never knew that the ability to recognize rhymes is a key to learning how to read words.

Or take games. Preschool and kindergarten teachers are masters at turning everyday tasks into fun games. But when teaching three-year-olds, you'd never make this type of game competitive, or focused on winning. Why? Because developmentally, most children this age would actually choose not to play a game rather than risk losing.

These are some of the things good teachers know about our children. Teachers have spent years learning about child development from people who have spent lifetimes studying it. The best early childhood teachers know who three- to six-year-olds are. They understand what you can expect from them and what's unreasonable, how they think, how they play, and how they learn.

Before getting into the classroom to learn the tricks good teachers use, we'll take a quick look at childhood development—the basics of how children grow, what you can expect when—and see how this knowledge can help you more easily use teacher tricks at home.

An understanding of child development helps a good teacher through her day. It helps her figure out the best way to get her students' attention; it shows her if a child's play is healthy or worrisome. And it explains why a teacher in a three-year-old preschool classroom would be relatively unfazed if one child bit another during a dispute over a toy—an incident that would be more disturbing in a kindergarten classroom.

Here are a few ways understanding childhood development can help you in day-to-day life with your child. These are based upon curriculum early childhood teachers use to teach prereading and premath skills with everyday activities.

Did you realize that when you...
- Teach your child to line up her shoes, you're helping develop the left-to-right eye sweep she'll need later as a reader?
- Help your child organize toys into bins and baskets, you're helping him develop the skills needed for visual memory of words during reading?
- Follow a calendar or schedule, you're working on the basics for telling time?
- Allow your child to set the dinner table, you're providing the spatial awareness needed to set up addition and subtraction problems later in math?

Here are some developmental milestones outlined by the American Academy of Pediatrics. These are excerpted from the AAP books, *Caring for Your Baby and Young Child: Birth to Age 5* and *Caring for Your School-Age Child: Ages 5 to 12*, which include charts that outline children's physical, language, and social milestones.

At age three, most children are able to:
- Imitate adults and playmates.
- Express affection openly.
- Understand the concepts of mine and yours, and his and hers.

- Hold a pencil or crayon and use it to make lines and circular strokes.
- Screw and unscrew jar lids, nuts and bolts.
- Follow a two- or three-part direction.
- Recognize and name common objects and pictures.
- Match an object in their hand to a picture in a book.
- Play make-believe with dolls, animals, and people.
- Sort objects by shape and color.
- Understand the concept of two.

You would want to talk with your pediatrician if your three-year-old:
- Is unable to communicate in short phrases.
- Has no involvement in pretend play.
- Fails to understand simple instructions.
- Has little interest in other children.

At age four, most children are able to:
- Engage in increasingly inventive pretend play.
- Be interested in new experiences.
- Cooperate with other children.
- Begin to negotiate solutions to conflicts.
- Copy a square.
- Draw a person with two to four body parts.
- Begin to copy some capital letters.
- Understand the concepts of *same* and *different*.

- Speak in sentences of five to six words.
- Tell stories. Recall parts of a story.
- Understand the concept of counting.
- View himself or herself as a whole person—with a body, mind, and feelings.

You would want to talk with your pediatrician if your four-year-old:
- Has difficulty scribbling.
- Shows no interest in interactive games.
- Ignores other children.
- Doesn't respond to people outside the family.
- Doesn't engage in pretend play.
- Lashes out without any self-control when angry or upset.
- Doesn't use sentences of more than three words.
- Doesn't use "me" and "you" appropriately.

At age five, most children:
- Want to please their friends and be like their friends.
- Are agreeable to rules.
- Are able to distinguish pretend from real.
- Tell longer stories.
- Like to sing, dance, and act.
- Use the future tense when speaking.
- Can copy triangles.
- Are able to print some letters.
- Can dress and undress without help.

- Can eat using a fork and spoon.
- Can count ten or more objects.

You would want to talk with your pediatrician if your five-year-old:
- Is extremely fearful or timid.
- Is extremely aggressive.
- Is unable to separate from parents without a major protest.
- Shows little interest in playing with other children.
- Refuses to respond to people in general, or responds only superficially.
- Rarely uses imagination or imitation while playing.
- Seems unhappy or sad much of the time.
- Doesn't express a wide range of emotions.
- Can't correctly give her first and last name.
- Doesn't talk about her daily activities and experiences.

Children Develop at Their Own Pace

While these guidelines outline milestones a child should reach by a certain age, it's easy to instead look at your friend's child or your child's classmate and say: "Hey, she's only three and she can already write her name! My daughter can barely print a letter!"

Linda DeMino Duffy is a San Antonio kindergarten teacher and the 2001 Texas State Teacher of the Year. She notes that parents often worry when their child can't do something her peers can do, such as print letters or add numbers, but says these struggles can be quite normal.

"Parents forget that sometimes. They look at their child and worry, 'She can't do that,' or 'She's having trouble with this,' when in actuality, the child's abilities are normal for this age group," she says. "Sometimes you just need to let it go, and remember that they're four or five years old. Give them time."

Mrs. Duffy notes that teaching standards also can ignore the fact that not all children develop the same skills at the same rates. Parents need to provide the support that can sometimes be lacking in a classroom and help their children recognize their unique strengths.

"We're putting kids in these classrooms where they're so academically pushed. Some kids are ready for it. But I was a kid who struggled to read, and I thought I was quite stupid. It's hard when you see someone else doing something so easily, and you're struggling with it.

"I think you need to look at your kids and help them feel special about where they are creative. They may be creative musically or mechanically. Everyone is gifted in some way. There are all kinds of giftedness. Everyone has their niche."

How Children Develop Socially Between Three and Five

Taking these developmental milestones back to the classrooms, why would a preschool teacher not be as alarmed by a three-year-old biting a playmate as a kindergarten teacher would if a five-year-old did the same thing? It's not simply because a five-year-old has better control over his emotions—children at five still have difficulty controlling anger and frustration, and they still lash out.

But remember that by age four, children are able to negotiate solutions, they have a clear sense of themselves as being distinct from someone else, and they have learned the basics of cooperating with other children. And while aggressive behavior is common among two- or three-year-olds, it starts to decline at age four. At four, a child has a clear understanding that some actions are just unacceptable—especially in some environments. And by five, children are very social; they are aware of friendships and want to please their friends and generally follow the rules.

So an angry five-year-old might stamp his feet and yell at his classmate: "That's not fair!" or "You don't know how to share!" or even "I'm never going to play with you again!" But he understands rules and social roles. Anger taken out in the form of kicking, spitting, or biting is not age-appropriate behavior for a five-year-old.

In understanding what is age-appropriate for a two- or three-year-old versus what's expected of a four- or five-year-old, it's important to remember that at two a child is still seeing the world almost completely in relation to himself. While a two-year-old can enjoy being with another two-year-old, he's just beginning to play with other children in a truly social sense—instead they might still play alongside each other or imitate each other. But by three, the same child is less self-centered and is actually interacting with other children.

The key to this change is simple, yet profound: He is realizing that not everyone thinks and feels exactly as he does. Interestingly, this is connected to the fact that by age three, children are able to sort objects—for instance, putting all the blue cars into one bin. As his social skills develop, he becomes able to transfer this "sorting" ability from objects to people. He begins to recognize how people are alike and how they are different. This frees him to then realize he is more drawn to some people than others—in other words, to start to desire friendships. Amazingly, by the time he is four, he's actually able to understand that he is a unique person, likable for his own traits and able to be a friend to someone else.

By the age of five, children set out with purpose to make friends. It is a deep-seated desire. They're able to talk about their thoughts and feelings—and to experience a sense of excitement and recognition when a friend shares the same feelings. While four- and five-year-olds are learning these skills and developing these abilities, they're acutely aware of what's expected of them in certain situations.

How Four- and Five-Year-Olds Show Respect and Responsibility

The National Association for the Education of Young Children (NAEYC) is the nation's largest professional organization for early childhood educators, focusing on improving educational programs for children through age eight. The NAEYC publishes a position statement titled "Developmentally Appropriate Practice in Early Childhood Programs Serving Children from Birth Through Age 8," with an accompanying textbook describing how the practices work in the classroom.

In terms of social development of three- through five-year-olds, the NAEYC textbook notes that teachers generally expect four-year-olds to be able to begin true give-and-take cooperative play, to become increasingly aware of what self-regulation behaviors are expected, and to seek to resolve negative interactions (even though they may lack the verbal skills to resolve all conflict).

In terms of expectations at home, this generally means that by four or five, a child is capable of beginning to show respect and responsibility. Mrs. Rice shares these expectations with interested parents of her kindergartners:

- By four or five, a child has developed a form of "adult talk" and "kid talk." When five-year-olds are talking to each other, there is a definite "kid" tone—sillier, slightly teasing, perhaps goofy. When talking to an adult, the same children may use a more reserved or even shy tone.

- A child this age is aware that name-calling does not cross over to adults. Children this age generally can see the difference between teasing and joking, versus being rude or name-calling. By four or five, it is inappropriate for a child to resort to name-calling with parents or caregivers.

- Four- and five-year-olds have begun to match this respect with places as well as people. Churches, restaurants, shopping malls, and libraries require certain behavior, and children this age realize their actions must match the context of where they are.

- A four- or five-year-old may show outbursts of anger and frustration—especially when tired or wound up—but is much less physically aggressive. Tantrums may involve arguing and shouting, but not hitting, biting, or spitting.

- Children this age understand the concept of ownership, and realize there are different rules when using toys or materials that belong to a playmate or school. Fights may break out over sharing items, but not over whom the item belongs to.

It's important to note that this *ability* to show respect and responsibility does not always translate into your child being respectful or responsible. In other words, just because your four-year-old knows how to behave at church, that doesn't mean she'll always behave well at church! But knowing what your child is capable of is the first step. The next—helping your child to listen, learn, and cooperate—will be detailed throughout this book.

When evaluating your child's social development, know that it's not all necessarily a forward progression. You'd like to think that once your three-year-old is willing to try new things, this sense of adventure will stay with him. Instead as some social skills develop, others may relapse. A three-year-old who is adventurous may be more timid at five, when he's discovering the world as a larger place and trying on social roles. A cooperative five-year-old may become argumentative at five-and-a-half, when his world is shifting from his parents being the center to friends and teachers taking on larger roles. These shifts are completely normal and expected (although you would never expect basic motor or verbal skills to be lost).

Do Parents Need Patience?

Of course! How else would they get through the dawdling, the demanding, and the general difficulties that accompany life with young children?

But Nancy Weber might argue that patience is one of the last things a good parent needs.

Mrs. Weber is an acclaimed former classroom teacher who is now a nationally known speaker and educational consultant. And she believes that people who work with young children need to understand them—not simply be patient with them.

Or to put it another way: You can get through your day with less frustration if you understand where your child is developmentally, rather than patiently enduring her behavior.

"When your reality does not match your expectations, you become impatient," she explains. "So if your expectations are unrealistic, you're going to spend a lot of time having to draw upon your patience."

On the other hand, if you know your child is not capable, developmentally, of sitting still for long periods of time, or of walking from point A to point B without stopping to examine every ant along the way, you'll hardly need patience at all. You already have understanding.

Mrs. Weber's points:

- Patient people may see themselves as martyrs, struggling through days of challenges imposed by young children. Understanding people try to celebrate children's growth and mostly enjoy their days together.

- People rely upon patience when their own needs are in conflict with the child's—for instance, your child needs to be active, but you need quiet. It can be easier to meet your child's needs with less frustration if you understand those needs.

Parents certainly may need to call upon their patience during demanding times. (Even Mrs. Weber recalls the time years ago when her young daughter defiantly pushed a bowl of cereal at her, splattering it all over her and her infant son, pushing her straight through understanding and past patience to anger.) But it's interesting to note how shifting your perspective from "patient" to "understanding" can change your reactions.

And as Mrs. Weber notes, if you rely upon patience to get through your days, there's a good chance you'll run out! Understanding will always be there.

How an Understanding of How Children Learn Guides Teachers

In addition to understanding developmental milestones, great classroom teachers rely upon an understanding of how the brain works and grows—or how a preschooler learns—to guide how they set up their environments and interact with students.

Some of the research that still guides teachers today dates as far back as the work of Russian psychologist Lev Vygotsky, who studied and detailed children's cognitive development in the 1920s. But the actual study of the inner workings of the brain is a newer field, and it wasn't until the 1980s that educators actively began translating the work of neuroscientists into actual teaching tools that could be used in the classroom.

While some "brain-based learning" can be controversial—does playing the right music help children learn math skills more effectively?—there are many time-tested and widely accepted understandings of how children learn that can be extremely helpful to parents at home.

Here are some of the most fundamental understandings that guide teachers in early childhood classrooms:

- Children need to feel safe in order to learn. This doesn't just mean physical safety, though that is essential. It includes the security of knowing they are cared for, that someone is watching out for them. And it means the safety of knowing what to expect next, and understanding what is expected of them. (Or in the words of the NAEYC's position statement on developmentally appropriate practice: "Children develop and learn best in the context of a community where they are safe and valued, their physical needs are met, and they feel psychologically secure.") By its nature, learning involves taking risks. Children who feel safe are much more likely to take these risks.

- The brain loves repetition—this is why children this age beg to hear the same story over and over, or sing the same song repeatedly, or ask "just one more time" after playing a favorite game. This repetition is key to helping a young child learn and process new information.

- With that said, the brain does crave new things. It needs challenges and novelty. This is why the book your three-year-old adored last week suddenly sits untouched on her shelf. Children are most likely to listen and learn when an activity is interesting and fun—but what was fun yesterday may be boring today. Little surprises can help get your child's attention.

- Young children learn how to do new things by watching and then *doing* them. They cannot learn how to do something new by simply listening to instructions. They need to actually practice or rehearse important activities.

- The brain learns best when it has a balance of quiet and active periods—after sitting or engaging in passive learning, children need to get up, run, jump, skip, and twirl. Movement stimulates the brain.

- The brain loves music and rhythm. Children can learn through songs and chants, which help the brain process and store information.

- A great way to reach a young child's brain is through the senses. The more senses involved in an activity or instruction, the more likely it is that the child will learn. Touch is huge for young children.

- Young children have a strong memory for stories. In contrast, they have limited memory for unrelated items—even practicing and using memory-association tricks won't help them remember random lists.

This understanding of how children learn underlies the best teacher techniques. It shows why silly songs can encourage a child, why a young child needs to run around after sitting still, why children need to practice skills we sometimes expect them to know instinctively. This understanding will be applied throughout this book as we describe the teacher techniques and adapt them for your home.

Three Guiding Principles

As we examine the techniques teachers use, it will be important to keep in mind both your child's stage of development and the basics of how she learns. But these are primarily meant as resources you can check periodically. They're intended to help you understand how your child grows and to be used as a reference when you have questions.

In applying the tricks good teachers use every day, the magic behind their secrets can be boiled down to these guiding principles:

- **Children ages three to six need to know what to expect next.** They need clear beginnings and clear endings to activities. Transitions are tough. Routine is their friend and partner—not the boring enemy many adults imagine it to be.

- **Kids this age need clear directions, broken down into manageable steps.** The more concrete or physical you can make a direction, the better they will hear and remember it.
- **For three- to six-year-olds, there's no such thing as too much fun.** At this age, a child's natural sense of play keeps her open to just about any task so long as it's approached with a sense of fun (and ideally, a time limit).

2

THE TEACHER SETS
THE TONE

Why It's Important to Respect Who You Are

One key we've already seen to making teacher tricks work at home is understanding where your child is developmentally—what he's ready for, what he can do, and what should be expected. The other key is knowing and respecting who *you* are—what you want as a parent, what works for you, and what just doesn't feel right.

The teacher sets the tone for her classroom. What works for one good teacher could fail miserably for another. The same group of students will respond differently depending upon the teacher who is leading them. And even good teachers have classes that are good in different ways—for example, one class may be more playful, another more focused.

The same is true at home. You set the tone for your home. No two good teachers are alike, and there's no single style for all good parents either.

If you adopt a style that isn't you—enforcing guidelines you don't believe in, or allowing negotiation where you feel there should be clear boundaries—you may see some changes in the short term. But it's unlikely you'll be able to apply the changes consistently, reliably, or confidently.

The key instead is to respect who you are and what's important to you as a parent—and then find or adapt the tools and techniques (in this book or elsewhere) to fit that.

When Mrs. Rice was a student teacher, she was told she'd never be an effective classroom teacher because her voice was too soft. She was assured that no young student would listen to her.

She didn't take voice lessons, practicing a loud and booming voice at home each night. Instead, she remained who she was, and found ways to get her students' attention without raising her voice. Today, she is proud when a student tells her parents, "Mrs. Rice is not a yelling teacher."

How Teachers Develop a Teaching Philosophy

Before earning their teaching degree, prospective teachers need to write statements defining their personal philosophies of teaching. These statements define their overarching goals for their classrooms—not the specific lessons they want to teach, but the type of teacher they want to be. They revisit this statement periodically, and share it anytime they interview for a job.

Mrs. Rice's teaching philosophy is: "I believe in promoting an inclusive education where children have an inherent right to develop intellectually, physically, socially, spiritually, emotionally, and culturally. This occurs in an environment that promotes active learning, critical thinking, healthy risk taking, and lifelong learning."

Kentucky kindergarten teacher Patrice McCrary describes her teaching philosophy statement as "one of the most simple and yet complex you will ever find." It simply reads: "I believe all children can and will learn with joy."

Texas teacher Linda DeMino Duffy's philosophy takes a different approach. It reads: "Teaching is a critical and challenging profession. If I were to write down the traits that a good teacher should cultivate and throw those words into a sieve they would include: responsibility, enthusiasm, self-confidence, tolerance, communication, trust, curiosity, creativity, selflessness, self-respect, and accountability. It is my feeling, however, that once you shake the sieve to strain away all but the most essential traits, you would find self-confidence, self-respect, and tolerance left remaining. To instill these traits in children is, in my opinion, the ultimate gift we can bestow upon them.

"Children need to be guided through a process. I help the children I teach to value success internally, and not just for what it will help them to gain from someone else. Learning can be made fun but sometimes it just requires hard work and determination. They need help in realizing that a failure is a good thing if you learn from your mistakes. That failure makes successes better and can help them strive to do better if they choose to persevere. Tolerance prepares them for an imperfect world, which will throw unexpected situations into their lives. It is essential that they learn to cope or deal with these kinds of situations."

Creating Your Own Philosophy Statement

You might want to take a few minutes to do this for yourself. First, think about these questions: What do you want for your children? How would you describe yourself as a parent? How will you measure whether you've succeeded?

Then write something down. Use your own words. You could write a few paragraphs, like Mrs. Duffy, or you could keep your statement short and simple—a single sentence (like Mrs. McCrary's) could be enough. For example: "I will try to create a home where children feel safe and loved. I will respect my children's abilities and limitations, and expect respect from them. I will provide my children with loving guidance and well-defined boundaries." Or simply: "My home will be loving and joyful."

Thinking about this at my own home, I struggled until one night when I was putting my youngest daughter to sleep. I play lullabies for her at bedtime, and the collection includes a gentle version of the folk song "Home on the Range." The line that captured me is: *"Where seldom is heard a discouraging word..."* I realized the phrase describes the home I envision for my kids.

By recognizing your own parenting philosophy, you may gain a new confidence in your parenting. No one has to evaluate or approve your statement. But now, when your sister-in-law tells you about the rules in her household, or your friend describes her system for getting her child to behave, or you read about a new parenting technique, you can simply ask yourself: Does this fit my parenting philosophy? If it does, consider trying it out. If it doesn't, move on.

And remember, you don't have to use every technique that sounds promising. Most teachers attend at least a conference or two each year, where they're bombarded with wonderful, inspiring ideas. Imagine if a teacher came back to school and tried to implement all the ideas she'd heard—rearranging her classroom, changing her curriculum, buying new materials, restructuring her grade book. It would be chaos. She and her students would be completely overwhelmed. No one would feel secure in the new environment. And the stress would undermine anything positive that could have come from a few changes.

So be willing to try new things. Be open to doing things differently. But know that the trick isn't to dramatically change who you are as a parent. Instead, find the tools and techniques that fit you best, then practice them and use them until they feel comfortable and work for you and your child. And if something doesn't work, feel free to adapt it or forget about it.

3

HELPING YOUR CHILD LISTEN AND FOLLOW DIRECTIONS

How Classroom Techniques Can Guide You

A good early childhood teacher would never walk up to a group of four-year-olds working on an art project and say: "Let's clean up, okay? It's time for lunch!" the way many parents might.

I used to give instructions such as these. And then the downward spiral would begin. My daughter, engrossed in her task and wanting to finish, would acknowledge me but hurriedly continue doing what she was doing. Or she negotiated with me. Thinking about what I needed to do next and worrying about how I'd get x, y, and z done, I would repeat myself and get frustrated. Or I'd engage in the negotiations, offering five more minutes, which turned into ten. Sometimes I gave up and began the cleanup myself. And I thought: "There has to be a better way."

Thankfully, there is. Before examining the techniques teachers use to get students to listen and follow directions, let's quickly review the three guiding principles that make teacher tricks work so well:

- Children ages three to six need to know what to expect next. They need clear beginnings and clear endings to activities.
- They need simple directions, broken down into manageable steps. The more concrete or physical you can make a direction, the better they will hear and remember it.
- Make it fun. A natural playfulness keeps young children open to just about any task approached with a sense of fun and, ideally, a time limit.

How can these guidelines help? How do classroom teachers use them so children listen to what they say and then follow their directions?

Good early childhood teachers provide clear and consistent cues to let children know when one activity is ending and another is about to begin. They make sure they have the children's attention *before* giving their directions. They break their directions down into clear and manageable steps. They use gestures and physical cues to emphasize their meaning, for example, pointing to the bin where the toys belong. And when appropriate, they use creative tricks to make everyday tasks fun.

If You Have More Than One Child

These techniques can be used for one child, several, or a large group. Be certain, however, to practice the techniques with all the children, and give them each individual attention. Offer plenty of praise and positive reinforcement. Try not to turn the techniques into a race or competition—praise each child for her progress, rather than comparing the children to each other.

Handling Transitions: The Key to Getting Through Your Day

The toughest parts of your day—the times when you're trying hardest to get your child to listen to you and follow your directions—are probably the moments known in early childhood classrooms as transitions, or the time you're moving from one activity to another.

Think about the transitions in your day: getting your child dressed and ready to head out the door, getting her to stop a project so you can go to the store, getting everyone to the dinner table, getting through bath time and bedtime.

While the act of moving from one activity to another may sound simple, transitions are actually the times when children are most likely to melt down into tears and tantrums, and the adults in charge are most likely to give in to their own anger and anxiety. Transitions probably account for the most frustrating, exhausting, or confrontational parts of your day.

Why?

No one likes to stop something they're enjoying or leave someplace they're comfortable to move on to something that has to be done or someplace they have to go. Young children don't switch gears easily. They don't have enough experience to know how to handle these changes. They also don't have control over when the changes will happen—or sometimes even an understanding of why they're happening.

Some kids feel frustrated at having to give up an activity they were enjoying. Others get angry. Some become fearful at having to move on to something else. Some feel all of this at once. And that's all just the natural difficulty of transitions. They're made even tougher if the child:

- Feels anxiety, because she doesn't know what to expect next.
- Is scared, because she's being yelled at or rushed, or senses that her mom or dad is anxious or disapproving.
- Feels out of control, because she's not prepared to move on.

Your job is to eliminate these sources of stress, respecting where your child is at and giving her the tools to move on. We'll start with the general guidelines to help your child to listen—how you can create and use consistent cues to get your child's attention, and how to give your directions clearly—and then move on to fun, classroom-based techniques for handling some of the specific transitions you face each day.

Getting Your Child's Attention

Remember to first get your child's attention and then speak *to* your child when giving directions. So often as parents, we try to get our children's attention by calling across the house while they're playing or watching television. Or we even speak with our backs to our children while we try to finish a task of our own.

On the other hand, when our children want our attention, they tug at us, they climb into our laps, they place themselves between us and whatever we're doing. They struggle to get and maintain eye contact. (Think about when you're on the phone and your child wants your attention.)

Follow your child's lead. Be physically in your child's presence before speaking. Speak to your child directly, making sure you have eye contact. Touch him on the shoulder, or hold his hand while speaking.

It may be helpful to create a "listen to me" signal that you can use routinely. This provides the cue to end an activity. This signal is best kept simple, but unique enough that it's associated with stopping and looking at you for further directions. Some teachers turn the classroom lights off for a moment. You might have a small bell or some wind chimes, or you might simply use a consistent verbal cue: "It's time to listen to me."

Whatever you choose, this process will work much better if you explain it first and practice it, at a time when you are both in a good mood and not rushed.

Patrice McCrary, who was named to the 2006 USA Today All-USA Teacher Team and was the 2003 Kentucky State Teacher of the Year, can get a roomful of chattering, playing five-year-olds to turn to her simply by saying in a soft voice: *"May I have your attention?"*

"I can't stress this point enough, though: This is a procedure we practice a great deal at the beginning of the school year," she explains.

Remember that this is how children learn. Teachers practice procedures like this in the classroom until they become natural. You need to practice at home as well. "When I ring this bell, that means I need to tell you something about what we're doing next. You need to put down whatever you're doing, and then look at me. Let's give it a try right now and see how it works."

Other Cues to Get Your Child's Attention

- Play a few notes on the piano.
- Strum some chords on the guitar.
- Play a kazoo.
- Turn off the lights.
- Turn off the television.
- Ring a bell.
- Play a music box (which also may have a visual element to draw your child in).
- Blow some bubbles.

Giving Your Directions: Make Them Simple and Fun

Once you clearly have your child's attention, it is time to give your instructions. If they have the time, some teachers find it best to further put the children in a listening frame of mind by beginning with a series of fun directions ("Touch your toes. Touch your nose. Touch your belly. Look at me.") or simply having them move from the activity that just ended to a new spot.

In Mrs. McCrary's kindergarten classroom in Kentucky, her favorite technique to get the children to sit quietly before giving her directions is to tell them: "Let me see if the magic works."

"For this one, I cover my eyes," she explains (though to be safe she discreetly peeks between her fingers), "then I count to three. By the time I get to three, I uncover my eyes and the children are all 'magically' on the carpet sitting criss-cross-applesauce. They love impressing me with the 'magic.'"

When you give your directions, remember they should be clear and manageable. Say exactly what you want to happen, broken down into steps. Rather than, "Clean up this mess," say: "Put all the cars into this bin then put it on the shelf in your bedroom."

Try not to ask a question when you mean to give a direction. In Mrs. Rice's classroom, she has often noticed parents asking children: "Would you like to come read now?" or "Would you like to do your project now?" Phrased as a question, you're giving the child a choice.

Before Giving Directions

- Play a singing game together—sing the alphabet song in very quiet voices, or sing "Itsy Bitsy Spider" as fast as you can.
- Do some simple stretches together. Sit on the ground and stretch out your legs, touch your toes, lean to the side.
- Play an echo game, where your child has to repeat your words, or clap a pattern your child has to follow.
- Play a mirror game, where your child has to mimic your actions.
- Get a flashlight and have your child follow its beam on a trail through the house to a different location where you then quietly tell her the directions.
- Simply announce cheerfully: "Come sit down over here while I tell you what we're going to do next." (The simple act of following your direction to move from one place to another will put your child in a listening frame of mind.)
- Use silly voices, such as a *slooowwwww* snail voice, a roaring lion voice, a purring kitten voice to give your directions.

When giving your child a task he needs to complete, instead try to use statements or commands. "We are going to the store. Please put on your coat and shoes," is clearer than: "Could you put on your coat and shoes so we can go to the store?"

And try not to end your directions with *"okay?"* This makes you sound indecisive and as though you're asking for your child's approval. Instead, end your directions with a nod or a smile as a cue that you are done talking. These cues help your child understand that what you are saying is important and that listening is important.

Some Pitfalls

So what were some of the pitfalls that trapped me when I cheerfully announced cleanup time and then let my frustration grow as cleanup didn't happen? For starters, as I've mentioned before, I failed to make it clear that while this project was over and something new was beginning, my daughter would be able to finish her work later. This is huge to a young child—we may know that when we stop our work, we'll be able to resume it again, but kids have much less control. They need to know you respect their work, and that they'll get a chance to finish.

This "you can come back to it later" signal needs to be concrete and reliable. It's not enough to say, "Oh, you can finish that later," because your child probably already knows that "later" often just doesn't come. You need a system—something simple, easy, and doable—that makes the process automatic. That's the beauty of Mrs. Rice's "Not Done" pouch, and other techniques for putting a project aside.

At my home, I also failed to make sure I had my daughter's attention *before* making my cleanup announcement. I could have told her, "I need to see your green eyes," as a cue for her to look at me, or touched her arm to get her attention.

And I needed to follow up with clear, understandable directions. To me, the cleanup was obvious: Put away the paints, pick up the papers, wipe up the mess. But it's not so obvious to a young child, who was immersed in creating something and now suddenly looks around at a mess and doesn't know where to begin. It's overwhelming. You need to be the one to break it down into manageable steps. Simple directions make it doable.

(We adults aren't that different. My daughter's school has a room that scouting troops use for meetings. Someone hung a sign on the door: "Scout troops, please clean up after using this room." Thankfully, someone had written under that: "Wipe down the tables. Sweep the floors.")

Adding a physical element to the directions makes them easier to remember. So when approaching cleanup at home, I could hold up

How Timers Work—And When They Don't

You can set a timer or establish a time limit when you begin everyday tasks or when you try out many of the activities presented in this book. It's important to know that this technique is meant to be fun, and to let your child know that the cleanup or other task won't last forever. It does not mean that you or your child should be rushing around madly, or creating more stress by worrying about beating the timer.

It's important that your child enjoys the timer, rather than being threatened by it. Set it for an amount of time that will allow him to successfully "beat" it, especially the first few times you use it. Or use a favorite song instead. Don't berate your child if the time is up and he isn't finished. And if your child intentionally dawdles or ignores the work so that the timer rings before the work is finished, accept that this isn't the right tool for you right now.

three fingers. "We're going to pick up the paints [*touch one finger*], put away the paper [*second finger*], and wipe off the table [*third finger*]." Or I could touch my daughter's shoulder while giving the directions, or point at or touch each thing I want her to accomplish (first the paints, then the paper, then the table).

And of course, from there, it's best to make it fun—or at least light-hearted. At my home, my cleanup efforts were undermined by the fact that I tended to pass my own anxiety and desire to rush on to my daughter. I'd already be stewing over how far behind we were and mentally listing everything I needed to get done, rather than taking it one step at a time. Instead of sighing heavily or pointedly grabbing the paint off the table, I could turn on some music, or set a timer.

Transitions at Home: Getting Up, Getting Going, Getting Settled

---

When tackling the transitions in your day, find the techniques that best fit you or most appeal to you. Remember, what works for one teacher marvelously could fail miserably in another classroom, if it doesn't fit who that teacher is and how she approaches her teaching. The same is true at home. If you're awkward singing a song, that will show. (My own children literally covered their ears and shouted, "I don't like that song!" when I tried my hand at singing instructions to a familiar tune.)

BOOKMARK IT!

AGES: 5–6

Materials: Strip of cardboard or poster board, markers, glue, scissors, hole punch, yarn, glitter, other decorations

Preparation: Create a large "bookmark" with your child by decorating the cardboard and tying a yarn tassel through a hole punched at one end. Show your child how a bookmark is used to hold your place in a book, so that you can pick it up again at the same place later.

What to Do: When you need to interrupt your child's play, say: "Let's put our bookmark here until we get back." Have your child place the bookmark on top of the toy, puzzle, project, etc. When the time is right, your child can resume where she left off.

"FINISH LATER" FOLDER

AGES: 4–6

Materials: Art portfolio, or two pieces of poster board and tape; markers, glue, decorating materials

Preparation: With your child, decorate the portfolio with your child's name, pictures, stickers, or other decorations. Or to make a portfolio, tape together the two short and one long sides of poster board, making a pouch. Decorate as desired.

What to Do: When your child must leave a project, have him put it into his "Finish Later" folder. Make sure the folder stays in the same place so your child can easily locate it, and be certain to give your child time to get back to his works in progress.

OUT TO LUNCH!

AGES: 3–5

Materials: A square of poster board, markers, ribbon, a hole punch

Preparation: Create an "Out to Lunch" sign with your child by decorating the poster board, punching holes at the top corners, and tying the ribbon through it.

What to Do: When it's time to stop your child's play for lunch or another activity, let your child hang the sign near his project area. Leave everything in place until it's time for your child to return.

Variation: Create a "Will Return Later" or a "Do Not Disturb" sign.

PUPPET PLAYMATES

AGES: 3–6

Materials: Sock, glue, buttons, wiggly eyes, felt or fabric scraps, pipe cleaners, markers

Preparation: With your child, attach wiggly eyes to the closed end of the sock. Add pipe cleaner whiskers and felt ears. Draw a mouth.

What to Do: Have the puppet creep out to give directions in a quiet voice.

Variation: Cut the finger from a wool or fabric glove. Use the finger piece, and draw or glue on eyes. Glue on felt or use markers to add colorful stripes down its body, to transform it into a caterpillar.

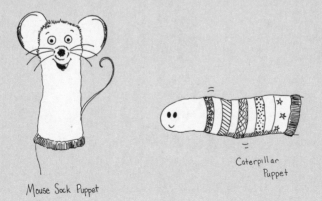

Mouse Sock Puppet

Caterpillar Puppet

MAGIC WANDS

AGES: 3–5

Materials: Stick or dowel (or chop sticks, or a nonbendable straw); felt or sturdy construction paper; ribbon or garland; glitter paint or fabric paint; scissors; glue, hot glue gun, or stapler

Preparation: Cut a star or heart shape from the felt or construction paper. Decorate it with the paint (for construction paper) or fabric paint (for felt). Attach ribbons or garland, if desired. Attach to stick with hot glue gun or stapler. Or attach strips of the garland to a stick or ruler with stapler or hot glue gun.

What to Do: Wave the magic wand then announce: "When I say abracadabra, you will..." then give your directions.

The techniques outlined through the rest of this chapter are simply tools, adapted from the tricks great teachers use in their classrooms. You may have to figure out the best way to use them in your own home. These suggestions may be adapted—feel free to experiment, mix and match, and add your own touch.

Starting Your Child's Day

Waking up in the morning and getting ready for the day may represent the most dramatic transition of the day. If you wake your child up each morning, consider your approach. You might consider waking your child with a gentle massage, rubbing his shoulders or back. Or you might open the shades, say good morning, and tell him what time it is, and then leave the room for him to awaken the rest of the way on his own, saying, "Come find me and tell me when you're awake."

If your child has extreme difficulty getting started in the morning and you're on a schedule where you need to all get out of the house early, you need to plan carefully. Be sure you're giving your child a few minutes to emotionally "catch up" after awakening before having to get out the door.

In Patrice McCrary's kindergarten classroom, she welcomes each child at the door every morning with a hug and a personal greeting. (At the start of the year, she gives each child the choice of a high-five, a hello-wave, or a hug for their morning greeting. This year, each chose a hug.) As she says: "I strongly feel that children need that individual interaction first thing in the morning. Don't you feel better when someone greets you with a smile when you walk in somewhere?"

At home, be aware of the tone you are setting for the day when you greet your child for the first time each morning. You may want to say: "We have to get going—sit down and eat breakfast," or "Hurry up and get dressed." But adding a simple morning routine of starting the day with a genuine smile, a hug, and some kind words can change the entire course of your child's day.

Here are some other teacher-adapted suggestions for waking your child in the morning. They all maintain the spirit of how teachers handle transitions in the classroom—with clear directions and a sense of fun:

- If your child sleeps with a stuffed animal, kneel by his bed and pretend to speak in the animal's voice, saying it's time to wake up and perhaps patting him gently with the animal's paw.
- Ring a small bell or play a music box.
- Provide a physical cue: Gently fold back one or more of the blankets that cover him and wish him a good morning.
- Gently rub a lotion with an invigorating smell, such as peppermint or citrus, onto her hands.
- Use a magic wand to magically awaken his feet, then his legs, then his back or stomach, then his arms, then his hands, then his chin, and finally his eyes. At the end, you could add something like: "When I tap your forehead, you're going to pretend you're a frog hopping from his lily pad bed."

If your child awakens early enough, or your morning routine is relaxed enough that you don't have to wake him up to get out of bed, still think about how you greet him to start the day. Offer a hug or gentle touch, a genuine smile, and a few words about how happy you are to start your day together. Be sure to get down on your child's level, making eye contact and using his name.

Getting Your Child Dressed

You should establish a clear routine for getting dressed and ready each day. As we'll see in Chapter 5, good teachers rely upon routines for getting through their days, and this is an area where a strong routine is a clear benefit at home. Perhaps you could pick out the day's clothes together the night before and leave them at the foot of the bed. Remember that if she's five or six, you could hand over much of the responsibility for getting dressed to her, rather than engaging in power struggles. You could consider setting a timer to show how long she has to get dressed, or play a music box or song—she has until the end to put on her clothes.

If your child is too young to dress herself, you still could involve her in the process and encourage her independence. Teachers use playful, imaginative games to help children through transitions like these. You might make a picture "shopping list" of clothes your child needs in the morning (either drawn or cut from a magazine or catalog) and leave it in a toy shopping cart or basket in your child's room each evening. When she wakes up, she can "shop" for what she needs, then bring her selections out to you to get dressed.

Or if you have a giant stuffed animal and don't know what to do with it, you can use it as a "dressing pal." Your child can pick out his clothes for the day, and then lay them on the stuffed animal, from head to toe. You can then check out the selection and help your child get dressed. Or you could lay out two outfits the evening before, one on each side of the animal. Your child could then choose the outfit he wants to wear.

The Morning Meeting

Most good preschool and kindergarten teachers start the formal part of their classroom day with a ritual called the morning meeting. This time is meant to introduce the day, provide some things to think about, and address any questions about the day. Usually, the teacher uses a calendar to show what day it is and what is planned, then gives the group a message about the day and asks the students for their input.

At home, you could have a simple morning meeting at breakfast. Introduce and discuss the events planned for the day. You could refer to a calendar. If there's a field trip at school, or you have a special outing planned, you'd discuss that. You could mention what you have planned for dinner when you return home. Always end your meeting by asking your child if she has any questions about the day.

Getting Out the Door

First consider any problems that are keeping you from getting out the door in a relaxed or productive fashion. Do you have enough time built into your schedule to allow your child to get dressed, eat breakfast, and be ready to leave on time? (We'll talk more about scheduling in Chapter 5.) Is your child anxious and upset about leaving you to go to day care or school?

In my house, we did pretty well getting up and ready, but somehow never managed to get out the door on time. During the most recent school year, my daughter was in second grade, and I had my four-year-old son and two-year-old daughter at home with me. Instead of getting routinely to the car to get to school on time, we inevitably were a flurry of shoes and coats rushing out just a minute or two too late.

At the time, I was working on this book and thinking about the school bell—how the children magically stop what they're doing and line up to go inside (or outside) when it rings. I wished for my own school bell in my living room to get the kids moving. Then I realized I was making this too complicated. We had plenty of digital alarm clocks, so I moved one into the living room and set the alarm for two minutes before we had to be in the car. It took only a few practices before the kids knew that when the alarm rang, everyone had to put on their shoes and get out the door.

Why did this work? Because I understood and mimicked the magic of the school bell. The school bell has a distinct purpose and only one job. It is reliable and it is meaningful. At home, I stuck to those principles. I didn't use the alarm to mean eight different things at six different parts of the day. And the tool had an important extra benefit: My daughter was less anxious in the morning, knowing she would get to school without having to hurry inside as the real school bell rang.

If your difficulties getting out the door aren't schedule-related, but more keyed to your child's anxieties about school or day care, you still could consider whether your routine of leaving for the day is adding to the stress. (We'll address handling separation anxiety when leaving your child at school at the end of this chapter.) Do you have a few quiet moments to spend with your child before heading out the door? Does she have the time to actually complete the tasks she needs to do? If not, you may need to adjust your morning schedule. Once that routine has been tweaked, here are some other strategies to lessen the "leaving home" anxieties:

- **Use humor.** Say something like: "When we get home, we have to remember to walk the elephant." Or look outside on a beautiful summer day and say: "Don't forget your snowpants. There's a blizzard out there!" Let your child have fun correcting you.
- **Make getting out the door fun.** An early childhood teacher might have her students pretend to be birds one day and fly out the door, then prowl like cats another day. You can: Trot like a horse, hop like a frog, waddle like a duck. If your child likes vehicles, you could drive out like a truck or chug like a train or zoom like a jet plane. The nature lover could glide out like a cloud or twirl like autumn leaves in the wind. You also could present fun physical challenges: Move like a pair of scissors or hop on one foot or pretend your legs are glued together. If you have an old skeleton key, you could pretend to use it to wind your child up like a toy and have her march out the door like a toy soldier.

EGG-CITING NEWS

AGES: 4–6

Materials: Plastic eggs, small slips of paper, markers

Preparation: On slips of paper, write ideas for fun activities that can be done when you return from work or your child's school day is done. You may want to draw a small picture of the activity. Suggestions include:

- "We'll watch a cartoon together before dinner."
- "We'll read a favorite story on the couch when we get home."
- "We'll make banana bread."
- "We'll share a cookie from the bakery."
- "We'll take a walk around the block after supper."

What to Do: Put the slip of paper with the fun activity into the plastic egg. Leave a new egg in your child's car seat or coat pocket each night. Then in the morning, he can look forward to leaving the house and discovering the fun you'll have later.

ROCK GARDEN

AGES: 3–5

Materials: 15–20 rocks of interesting colors, shapes, and sizes

Preparation: Clear a small area of the garden, grass, or flower bed for a rock garden. Make sure it is a place you pass each day on your way to the car, bus, or sidewalk.

What to Do: Every morning when your child is ready to leave, give her a small rock to place in the garden as you walk past. Watch your garden grow as the weeks go on and take occasional pictures of your child by the garden.

Variations: Make a sticker book to keep by your child's car seat or by the door. Every morning when your child is ready to leave, give him a sticker to add to the book. When the book is full, plan a fun activity.

For a special occasion or during an unusually stressful week, lay out a trail of flower petals leading your child to the car or sidewalk where you've left a packet of seeds you can plant together that evening or weekend.

PET PLAN

AGES: 4–6

Materials: Paper, markers, picture of family pet

Preparation: With your child, create a checklist for saying good-bye to your family pet. Write these down on a piece of paper with pictures. Add a photo of the pet. Suggestions for the list include:

1. Give Fluffy a treat.
2. Give Fluffy a good-bye pat.
3. Bring Fluffy a special pet blanket or pillow.
4. Turn on a radio or a light for Fluffy.
5. Remind Fluffy of your return. ("We'll be home at four thirty.")

What to Do: Each morning before leaving, have your child go through the list, checking off items as she completes them.

Interrupting Play

When you need to interrupt your child's play to do something else, you should keep in mind that his play is important to him. We'll address this more in Chapter 8. But for now know that while we may think, "He's just playing. He can always go back to what he's doing," the truth is that children become immersed in play, like adults become immersed in tasks that are important and meaningful to them. Play has stages and levels. Being interrupted from play can be likened to being interrupted from sleep.

In Mrs. Rice's classroom, when she has to interrupt a child's play, she acknowledges the interruption and tries to integrate the play into it. For example, she might ask the child to "drive your car over to the parking garage [the table]" to do the new activity. She could ask children in the playhouse to bring their babies over to her day care, where she can watch them in a nearby crib or high chair while Mom or Dad (the student) works with her.

At home, you could ask your child to park her toy car in the hallway "garage" while she cleans up her bedroom floor. Or you could roll her dolls over in a stroller to watch while she is getting dressed and brushing her teeth, then allow them to sit at the table while she eats breakfast.

Running Errands and Waiting

Simply doing the "stuff" of everyday living—going to the grocery store, stopping at the post office, taking the pets in for their annual checkups—can be challenging with a young child. Here are some ideas to help these times go more smoothly.

- If you're leaving to run an errand, occasionally make a game of it by giving your child an item or two that serve as clues to your destination—you could give a canceled stamp if you're stopping at the post office, a dog treat if you're going to the pet store or veterinarian, or some coupons for the grocery store. Have him guess where you're going.
- Understand that children simply aren't good at waiting. The longer the wait, the more likely they'll become restless or behave badly, so consider finding a way to engage your child and have fun with the time. While it's best to be prepared with small toys or activities (even a small rock can be fun to play a "Guess Which Hand It's In" game), you could simply practice noticing details. You might examine a spot on the wall, a section of sidewalk, part of a tree—any small area you normally wouldn't look at closely— and take turns describing it.

Making Cleanup Time Fun

When it's time to clean up, try to maintain a spirit of playfulness. Don't forget to establish eye contact before giving a direction. You may want to guide your child with a gentle touch on her shoulder. Make up and use cleanup signals: Ring a bell, or use a triangle or a kazoo, or play a few notes on the piano.

Here are some other classroom-based ideas for making cleanup time go smoothly:

- Offer fun tools—for instance, salad tongs to pick large items off the floor, tweezers for tiny ones. Or put everything in a toy dump truck and drive it to the appropriate room. Wrap masking tape around your child's fingers, sticky side out, so she can use it to pick up small bits of trash. Or use a lint brush for this, perhaps even adding vacuum cleaner noises.

- Make your child his own personal cleaning basket, complete with a feather duster or spray bottle and paper towels. Let him decorate it.

- If your cleanup time is relaxed rather than hurried, you could play pretend games—How do you think the mouse family would clean up their hole? How would the bird family clean up their nest? How would the bear family clean up their cave? (Be prepared for some silliness here, and don't try this one if you want to get the cleanup done quickly.)

- When you're about to do something not-so-fun, announce the next fun thing you'll do. "After we put away our toys, we're going to go outside and check the mail." Or emphasize the positive to come. "We'll have more time to play outside because we're doing such a good job putting this all away quickly."

In her California kindergarten classroom, Susie Haas-Kane has a small music box she uses at cleanup time—the idea is to have the children clean up quietly and quickly while listening to the music. If there is still music playing once the cleaning is done, everyone gets a small treat.

For parents wanting to use a music box for cleanup time at home, she notes that a key is to make a big deal out of winding it up "new" each morning with your child. That way, they're already excited by the idea, and will more readily know what to do when you bring out the music box and announce cleanup time.

Handling Bedtime

Like waking up in the morning, going to bed at night can be a dramatic and difficult transition. The key to helping it go smoothly is to develop and follow a relaxing, consistent routine you use every night to build toward bedtime. Preschool and kindergarten teachers sometimes use relaxation techniques to prepare reluctant sleepers for naptime. They build a routine into their day so the children are able to wind down before naptime, and usually dim the lights and play relaxing music as cues that it's time to rest.

To help move toward bedtime at home, you could create some fun and relaxing rituals such as:

- Sprinkle a bit of "sandman's dust," or baby powder, over your child before sleep.

CLEANUP INSPECTOR

AGES: 3–5

Materials: Magnifying glass, white gloves, note pad, pencil

Preparation: Explain that the "Cleanup Inspector" will check to be sure toys are put away, the floor is cleaned up, etc. This will create a sense of excitement and anticipation as your child cleans.

What to Do: As Cleanup Inspector, your child should use her magnifying glass or put on her white gloves and examine the cleanup! She might look for all the things that are well done. She can draw a smiley face on the notepad and leave the paper in well-cleaned areas. She should note any areas that need more attention.

Variation: A parent can use a puppet as a Cleanup Inspector.

THE QUEEN RULES

AGES: 3–5

Materials: None.

Preparation: None.

What to Do: Open a bedroom or closet door and come out as the royal queen or king. Simply assign tasks in a royal voice—wipe off the table, pick up papers, put away cars, etc. Offer comments and praise in your royal voice. When jobs are done, you could use your royal voice to make helpers honorary knights, princes, and princesses.

Variation: Use a play telephone and pretend that "Mrs. McGillicudy" has just called to say her child is already cleaning up his mess. Challenge your child to race Mrs. McGilllicudy. Call Mrs. McGillicudy back when cleanup is done to describe your child's fast and efficient work.

HERE'S YOUR TICKET

AGES: 4–6

Materials: Pencil, slips of paper

Preparation: On small slips of paper, write tasks that you would like to be completed in the house. Draw a small picture to go with each one.

What to Do: Give the slips to your child. Read them together and explain the job or task on each one. When your child finishes a task, he can give you the corresponding slip. When all are turned in, your child can get a "ticket" for a trip to the playground, a back rub, or a special game time.

SING A SONG OF CLEANUP

AGES: 3–5

Materials: None.

Preparation: None.

What to Do: To give cleanup time a spark, try singing a song as you clean up a room or area. Some suggestions:

"I'm Bringing Home a Baby Bumblebee" tune
We're cleaning up the living room 1–2–3
Putting all the toys away you see.
We're cleaning up the living room yesiree!
Very neat and tidy!
(cleaning up the bedroom, putting all the clothes away; cleaning up the yard, putting all the balls away, etc.)

"Wheels on the Bus" tune
The blocks on the floor go in the box
In the box
In the box
The blocks on the floor go in the box
Whenever we clean up!
(dolls go in the crib, books go in the case, crayons go in the bin, play dough goes in the can, etc.)

- Rub "sleep potion," or body lotion, gently on her arms and legs, as a gentle massage.
- Practice muscle relaxation techniques and visualization exercises. (For more on this, see Chapter 9.)

Once your child is tucked into bed, you could:

- Offer a gentle back rub, face rub, or head rub.
- Play soft music.
- Whisper a word of encouragement or special message.

Handling Separation Anxiety

If your child has difficulty separating at school or day care, respect his feelings but don't linger over them. Show confidence that your child can handle this. Children pick up very quickly on their parents' own doubts, so be positive.

Mrs. Haas, whom we met earlier this chapter, is a kindergarten teacher who has been inducted into the National Teachers Hall of Fame. She is the 1999 California State Teacher of the Year, a 2000 Disney Teacher Award honoree, and a nationally recognized literacy consultant. She says there generally are two types of children who cry when left at preschool or day care, and each should be dealt with a little differently.

"The first child doesn't want to be there. So they have the tears, they're crying, but they're angry," she explains. "That child, at some point, is going to make a move of some little kind to join the classroom. Then as a teacher, you're going to say: 'Oh my gosh, I'm so proud of Susie.'

"The other child is truly afraid. This child needs lots of tenderness. As a teacher, you're going to let this child sit on your lap, maybe hold your class mascot.

"For parents of the first child, they need to explain to Johnny that this is his job, he needs to come to school. He's not really afraid—he just doesn't want to be there. You can tell the difference—it's so easy. It's a child whimpering versus a child with a look on his face that says: I'm not going to be here!

"But for both children, the parents need to be firm. With the frightened one, the parent should not hug or hold the child too much, because this just plays into the child's fears. What they have to do instead is be very stoic: 'There is no reason for crying. You're in a safe place, with a safe teacher.'"

Some suggestions for the child who has difficulty separating:

- Before dropping her off, try saying good-bye with a statement that includes the past, present, and future parts of your day: "I had a lot of fun eating breakfast with you this morning. I know you're going to do great at school. When I pick you up, you can tell me all about your projects, and then we'll make paper airplanes together."

- Your good-bye should include a brief physical element—a kiss, a touch on the shoulders, a high-five. You might make up your own handshake to use at good-bye time—it could include a clap, snap, or behind-the-back motion.
- To help your child bridge the gap between home and school, you could attach a photo keychain to your child's backpack zipper with a picture of your family or family pet, or slip a laminated photo into her pocket or cubby.

When Mrs. Haas first meets new kindergarten students and their parents, she introduces them to a good-bye ritual called "the kissing hand," based on the book *The Kissing Hand*, by Audrey Penn. The parent kisses the child's palm, then tells her if she feels lonely, she can hold the hand to her heart or cheek to feel her parent's love.

Although Mrs. Haas's own sons were already ten and seven when this book came out and she began using it in her classroom, she did use "the kissing hand" with her sons occasionally when they seemed lonely or anxious during good-byes.

Then came the day her oldest son, Brian, headed off to college.

"He's all packed, his car is filled to the brim, he's sitting in the front seat saying good-bye," Mrs. Haas recalls. "I'm in the garage with tears running down my cheeks, happy but sad."

Then, as he pulled away, Brian stopped his car and ran to his mother. He took her hand, spread open her fingers, and kissed her palm.

"He told me I'll always be close to him," Mrs. Haas says. "I'll never forget that day."

Good-bye rituals may not always feel like they work—especially when your child is still crying or clinging when you leave. But they are meaningful and important, and they work in ways you may not immediately see or understand.

4

ORGANIZING
YOUR HOME

How Classroom Organization
Techniques Can Help at Home

Standing in my daughter's kindergarten classroom, cheerfully decorated and neatly organized, I was most struck by how simple it felt.
Over here, a place to play with blocks, there a play kitchen, here a
comfy reading section. It all conveyed a kind of "A place for everything and everything in its place" feel, but not in a stifled or demanding way. It simply felt comfortable and encouraging.

While I certainly didn't want my home to *look* like a kindergarten
classroom, I did want it to have that same safe and cheerful feeling.
Looking around Mrs. Rice's classroom, I realized that one of the secrets
behind the magic she worked every day was right there in the environment. Her room was peaceful and organized enough to give her

students the security young children crave, but not so organized or perfectly arranged that a child would feel uncomfortable taking a toy off a shelf or building a tower of blocks.

Your home, of course, is very different from a preschool or kindergarten classroom. The classroom is arranged almost entirely for the comfort and needs of young children, whereas your home needs to be comfortable to everyone who lives there. The classroom will always be used by preschoolers or kindergartners, but your own children will soon grow out of their early childhood years. And the classroom is simply a place to work and play, while your home has to support a whole variety of other functions.

However, by following some basic concepts used by early childhood teachers, your home can be like a good classroom in the most important way: When anyone enters a good classroom, they immediately feel welcomed and intrigued. A good classroom makes you want to spend time there. It makes you feel comfortable, while still challenging or stimulating you. Your home can do this, too, for both the children and the adults who live there.

Good early childhood teachers plan their classrooms so that their students are able to move through the room learning and exploring, without the teacher's constant intervention or guidance. The environment itself supports the children's work or play, allowing them to grow and explore.

This is a terrific concept to transfer to home. You can create your home environment in such a way that your child will be able to move through her days, playing and exploring, without the need for you to constantly guide her activities or correct her. You'll do this not only by organizing your home, as we discuss in this chapter, but also by structuring your time and creating a good set of basic ground rules (Chapters 5 and 6), in much the same way a good teacher does for her classroom.

It will not be necessary to make your home "perfect." It does not need to be expertly arranged, it should not be designed solely around the needs of your child, and it does not need to be filled with expensive organizational systems. Your goal is simply to make your home peaceful, accessible, and comfortable for everyone in your family. To help, we'll examine the elements a kindergarten teacher considers while setting up her classroom, and show you ways to adapt them to your home.

The Physical Space

Kentucky teacher Patrice McCrary notes that when adults step into her classroom, they often say, "I wish I could go back to kindergarten and be in this room."

Primary colors are everywhere, though a deep blue is dominant. At the core of the room, the students sit on an oval-shaped ABC rug, arranged in front of a white wicker rocker. Scattered around the room are comfy, child-sized chairs and even a child-sized recliner.

"I believe children need a variety of seating areas while they're at school—or at home," Mrs. McCrary explains.

Student work hangs from the ceiling attached with a colorful clothespin and the student's name. Every student has work on display at all times. The room includes the home living area (which has a variety of dress-up clothes, a kitchen set, a baby bed and dolls, tools, a cash register, a telephone, and more). Next is a long bookshelf that houses tubs of books categorized by authors and interests. There is a writing center, and an art center on wheels that can be moved to any table. On a large shelf jutting out from the wall are two sections devoted to math materials, and one to puzzles and games.

"*Everything* in our room is accessible to the children," Mrs. McCrary notes.

Looking at the Physical Space of Your Home

When evaluating the physical spaces of your home, the most important questions to ask are:

- Are there areas for your child to play? Ideally, there should be at least one open area where a child can play with blocks or other "creating" toys as well as one or two smaller spaces for imaginative play or quiet activities.

- Does each area serve its own purpose? Even if you have a small living area, you should distinguish spaces in some way by function: We prepare and eat food here, we sleep here, we spend time together as a family here. While the spaces for these functions can overlap, they should exist.
- Is there a space for each child to call her own? This could be a bedroom, or a portion of a bedroom, or even space in the living room, but it should be a place where each child is able to relax and feel she is in her own place.

You also should consider whether your spaces are child-friendly or accessible enough so your child can easily take part in the day-to-day tasks of family life. In the classroom, everything from the sinks to the chairs is child-sized and accessible. At home, this wouldn't make sense. But it does make sense to make small changes to allow your child to function easily in your home.

For instance, you could:

- Install large double hooks, like those used for classroom cubbies, in the hall closet where your child could easily hang his own jacket and backpack.
- Place a basket or bin on the floor under each hook to keep hats, gloves, and scarves near their separate owners. (If floor space is unavailable, mesh lingerie bags with draw string or zippered tops work well to store and hang small outerwear pieces.)

- Use low closet rods to help your child hang up and choose his own clothes in his closet.
- Install hooks on the back of a bedroom door to hang clothes or pajamas.
- Store toys on low shelves or in areas that your child can reach himself.
- Provide plenty of small boxes for storage.
- In the kitchen, you might:
  - Have a stool so he can help with dishes at the sink, or mixing at the counter.
  - Store unbreakable plates and cups in a lower cabinet, so your child could set the family table alone.
  - Allow your child access to a low cabinet with wooden spoons and plastic bowls for mixing.
  - Provide a child-sized broom in a cleaning closet.
- In the bathroom:
  - A stool helps a child more comfortably reach the toilet and sink.
  - A cabinet or low towel rod can store towels and washcloths that are easily accessible.

Get down on your child's level to see whether it will work—can your child reach the hook to hang his coat? Can he get clothes off the rod in his closet? Can he reach the shelf where his toys are stored without having to climb?

The Items Within Each Room:
Organizing Your Stuff

The thing that most stands in the way of creating a peaceful and organized environment is, simply, the *things*. Things seem to multiply in places with children, and keeping them all organized and accessible can sometimes feel impossible.

The key questions to consider when looking at your child's possessions and how they're organized are:

- When the time comes to put each thing away, is there a place for it? This is perhaps the heart of organizing spaces with young children. If something doesn't have a home, make one for it. Otherwise, there's no way for your child to put things away and keep them organized.

- Are most of the items my child uses on a daily basis accessible to her? Your child should be able to independently choose what she wants to play with, and put it away when she's done. (This also goes for personal care items, such as her toothbrush, towels, pillows, and the like.)

- Does she have too many or too few choices of playthings? Too many choices can be paralyzing for a child looking for something to play with. Too few make them all seem tedious and boring. If your child has too many toys, consider setting up as system of "rotating" the toys so some are put away and others brought out on a regular schedule.

Classroom Techniques for Organizing Stuff

Mrs. Rice uses several systems to organize toys and control the clutter in her classroom, including several personal storage areas for each student. In the hall, children have individual lockers where their coats, backpacks, snacks, and lunches are stored. Within the classroom, each child has a box of daily supplies—pencils, crayons, scissors. Hanging on each chair is a small plastic backpack where children store water bottles, tissues, and other personal care items.

The children learn that each of these personal supply areas holds specific items. They also learn, through putting items back in the correct spaces every day, that materials are easy to find, are rarely lost, and stay in good shape—unbroken and unharmed by the daily passage of feet and hands.

In Texas teacher Linda DeMino Duffy's classroom, toys are stored on shelves with a picture of the toy taped to the spot where it belongs. Toys with lots of pieces are placed in buckets labeled with a picture of the toy that belongs in it—the same picture is on the shelf where the bucket belongs.

"This helps promote independent cleanup without a lot of direction," Mrs. Duffy notes. "Sometimes kids get too dependent on the directions given to them by an adult. The pictures help them to be more independent and to get used to putting their toys away in an orderly fashion."

Clutter control in the home can be based on these classroom ideas. But organizing works best when children first realize *why* it is important to keep things organized. You and your child can look at a broken toy along with a well-cared-for toy and discuss which one would be more fun to play with. Try to build a puzzle with a few pieces missing and talk about how frustrating it feels. Or you could bring out a game that is not played with because it has missing pieces. Allow your child to come up with her own ideas about why toys should be organized and put away. This will increase her awareness and sense of responsibility for keeping things organized.

Allowing children to be involved in setting up the actual organization is also important. You might take pictures of your child playing with different toys, and then allow him to put these pictures on the bins that contain these toys. Or your child could choose colored containers for different toys. You might spend time together decorating shoe boxes to store toys.

But do not try to come up with a new organizational system overnight. Take it one step at a time, being certain to first get rid of the items that aren't used, aren't loved, or are simply broken beyond repair. From there, spend some time observing where your child naturally uses and keeps his toys, and try to arrange the storage places around those patterns.

About once a month, Mrs. Rice reevaluates her classroom environment, looking at each item and asking: Is it being used, or is it in the way? You could do the same at home, to help keep your organizational systems on track and reduce future clutter.

Paper, paper, everywhere!

For student papers that are coming into the classroom—homework and notes from home—Mrs. Rice assigns each student an office tray on a table near the classroom door, where students empty their folders each morning.

At home, the sheer amount of paper coming into your home can become overwhelming. Do not try to keep it all. You could buy an office supply tray, where your child can empty her folder at the end of the school day, allowing you to go through the papers later in the evening. Then you could return the items that need to go back to school—signed permission slips, completed homework—to the tray for your child to put back in her backpack in the morning. (This also encourages your child's self-sufficiency—there's a system in place that makes it easier for her to pack her own backpack, and she's doing it herself.)

By preschool, children can begin making decisions on what school projects or artwork they would like to save. An accordion-type folder works well for storing treasured keepsakes. You could buy one at the beginning of each new school year, and label it with the year to keep the clutter of saved school papers to a minimum.

Decorating: Adding the Personal Touches

In Illinois, kindergarten teacher Randy Heite's room starts out each fall as a pretty boring-looking place. Which is somewhat amazing, because Mr. Heite's room is probably one of the most fun, adventurous, child-centered places around.

Mr. Heite came to teaching in a roundabout way. After graduating from a vocational high school, he ended up doing volunteer work in New Guinea, living among various tribes. After long days of construction work, he spent his free time hanging out with the tribal children, learning from them how to prepare bat over an open fire and teaching them how to make sandals. He discovered his calling as a teacher, and pursued a teaching degree when he returned home. In 2003, Mr. Heitie was recognized as a Disney Teacher Award honoree.

When adults enter Mr. Heite's kindergarten classroom, they tend to stop in their tracks, almost transformed into kindergartners themselves. Over the course of the school year, his classroom gradually grows to include two 75-gallon aquariums—one saltwater and one freshwater—an iguana, a turtle named Maxie, a bearded dragon, geckos, trees, a woodshop, a potting table, a GrowLab, a play kitchen, and even an old-fashioned milkshake maker.

Mr. Heite believes that even young children need to have ownership in their environment. To make that happen, he starts the school year with a room that's almost empty—"plain and simple." He takes down all the posters, and the animals are added one at a time throughout the school year, as the children learn how to take care of them.

At the start of the year, each child is assigned a letter of the alphabet to "teach" the class, and they make a poster introducing their letter. These are added to the classroom as decorations, and add splashes of color. Later in the year, they're each given a large piece of felt during parent conferences, and given directions to create a family banner.

They sew or paint symbols onto their banner, and these soon decorate the classroom in a circle of banners.

By midway through the year, the classroom is buzzing with activity and fun. But the children each helped create it—and they can see themselves in it. And to Mr. Heite, that makes all the difference in the world.

When decorating at home, you want your child to similarly be able to see herself in her environment. For example, a child's bedroom space should fit her personality. Your child's space should include open areas on walls or shelves for displaying pictures or artwork. Your child's space should be inviting and pleasant to her.

Your child's mark, or presence, should also be visible in most of the living areas of your home, though in a quieter way. When decorating, you could incorporate elements of her past—small framed pictures of her as a newborn baby on a bookshelf, her first drawing framed in your bedroom, the bouquet of paper flowers she made in preschool as your Mother's Day present sitting atop your desk. These show your child is valued in the family, and help her gain a sense of how she's growing and changing.

While many kindergarten classrooms are brightly decorated, this is not a requirement for children's spaces. As Mrs. Duffy notes: "I think it is important to keep decorations basic and not too cluttered. A child who has trouble focusing on her work needs a bright, happy environment but not something that will make her head spin. I happen to like blue, so I have a lot of background areas that are covered in a dusty blue color or a darker blue."

Stephanie Seay, the 2006 South Carolina State Teacher of the Year, uses natural colors and material in her kindergarten classroom whenever possible. She uses woven seagrass baskets to store items. Her play centers include natural and homemade items—for example, pieces of tree limbs that have been cut and sanded to use in the block area.

"I think sometimes in early childhood, it's very easy to bombard children with primary colors. In a sense, this just undermines the depth of what they can appreciate," she says.

The Teacher's Desk: Why Some Areas Can Be Off-Limits

While you want to keep your child's needs in mind when organizing and decorating your home, it's important to also recognize that it's okay to have some areas that are not child-friendly—even spaces that do not consider the needs of your child at all. In an early childhood classroom, this might be known as the "Rule of the Teacher's Desk."

The teacher's desk is set up for the convenience of the teacher, not her students. In Mrs. Rice's classroom, children must ask before they look at the photos and other decorations on her desk. They must ask before using the tape or stapler or pencil sharpener on her desk.

As she explains: "I tell the children that my desk is a place where I can keep my favorite things—I mention my photos, special knick-knacks, pictures drawn for me. I mention that it is a place where I feel good going—I can eat lunch there or work quietly while the children are away. I make it clear I may invite children to my desk, but they should not be playing behind it or moving things around on it."

In your own home, your "teacher's desk" might be your bedroom, a formal living room, or a home office. These areas can be off-limits to your children—the rule might be: No one is allowed in Mom's office when the door is closed, or they might be allowed there with "no touching" or "ask first" rules. Theses guidelines help your child understand that everyone has things that are special or important to them, and establishes boundaries that help her understand respect for property and taking care of personal items.

You can explain the rules with comments similar to the ones Mrs. Rice uses in her classroom: "This is my work spot," or "I need to keep my things safe here," or "I feel good when I can be in this spot." You might want to invite your child to your spot—for instance, to build a puzzle together at your desk, or to respectfully look at special items on your dresser.

But remember that your home is also meant to be safe and comfortable for *you*. You should have places where your things are safe and some areas that are yours to enjoy, knowing your belongings and privacy will be respected.

5

ORGANIZING
YOUR DAYS

Helping Your Day Run Smoothly

Daily schedules keep great early childhood classrooms running smoothly. Good teachers also rely upon routines, checklists, and calendars to help their students know what to expect next, feel some control over their day, and experience less fear or anxiety. Classroom

> ### If You Have More Than One Child
>
> The tools described in this chapter remain the same, though you should be certain to include each child's needs and preferences in creating your schedules and routines, and of course, be sure household jobs are distributed fairly.

jobs are assigned so the students take responsibility for their environment, and the teacher is not left doing all the work.

We'll take a look at each of these tools, and how you can adapt them to your home.

How to Create a Workable Schedule

Schedules give the day an underlying structure. They help teachers—and parents—make sure that the things they need to get done actually happen. Early childhood teachers use schedules to keep children on track and give them a clear sense of "what happens next." Schedules help lessen the stress of transitions.

At home, I had never been a big fan of written schedules. I knew that no matter how hard I tried, I'd never be able to precisely stick to the schedule—and the things I didn't get done today would somehow have to be moved to tomorrow. Schedules also seemed controlling and rigid, like they'd suck all the fun out of a day that otherwise would have promised all sorts of possibilities. And I was uncomfortable with the idea of someone walking into my home and seeing an hourly listing of our day's plans posted in the kitchen.

But then, speaking with good early childhood teachers, I learned that a schedule could be a detailed account of your day's activities or it could be a general guideline for how your days unfold, depending upon what's most comfortable and natural to you. It could be written each morning on a dry-erase board posted in your kitchen for everyone to consult, or

When good teachers schedule their days, they recognize one important concept: Everything takes longer than they'd expect. You don't want a schedule that keeps you rushing around and worried about staying on track, or one that dooms you to failure. Be sure to schedule extra time around activities. If your child needs to be at day care at 8 a.m. and it usually takes 20 minutes to get dressed and eat breakfast, plan on at least 25 minutes to get dressed and eat breakfast. It's better to have a few extra minutes to relax than to rush around trying to get out the door on time.

it could simply consist of some notes scrawled in a personal notebook to see how your daily life matches up with your life's priorities.

The key to making a schedule work is keeping it in perspective as a *tool*—it is something to help you run your day, not something that actually controls the day's activities. A schedule should not force you to rush or worry. It should not be so rigid that you or your child are lost if you're not following it precisely. In order to be effective, it needs to be both predictable and flexible. The point of developing a schedule is to make sure you are doing the things that you value.

Regardless of how you want your final schedule to look and how you plan to use it, you should approach creating a schedule by asking yourself:

- What few things *have* to happen each day? These might simply be things like getting dressed in the morning, preparing meals, and getting your child to sleep at a reasonable hour each night. They likely include your child going to school or day care. Depending on your child's age, they might also include homework time or a nap. These are things that need generally to happen at a certain time, and the rest of your day must fit around them.

- What are some things that are very important priorities for your family, things that you really want to do every day they're possible? In my house, they include having outside playtime and reading time together. Your list might include time with your child for crafts, sports, cooking, or building. Write these down, or the opportunities to actually do them might simply slip away.

To get a true feeling for how much time you have in your days and where you have free time or conflicts, it's helpful also to consider:

- What few things need to get done around the house each day to keep it feeling peaceful and productive? They might include making the beds, washing the dishes, wiping down the bathroom, or doing a load of laundry.
- What things do you need to do to take care of yourself? If you don't include these, there's a good chance they'll get lost among everyone else's needs.

Next, you might think about the things you'd *like* to include both with and without your child, and see how these fit in. Perhaps you'd enjoy taking an evening walk alone after dinner, or feeding the birds together in the morning before breakfast. Maybe you want to plant a

It's Okay If Your Schedule Looks Empty

As you review your daily schedule, you may look at it and say: "You mean this is all I get done in a day?" Don't despair. If that's the first thought that jumps out at you, this is actually a good sign.

Remember: Young children need large blocks of time that are basically unstructured and unproductive. These periods of time allow them to make connections and learn concepts. Your child should not be spending her days going from one scheduled activity to another. She needs time to discover on her own the things that interest her. Her brain needs time to process and make connections. Simply put, she needs time to be left alone.

"Kids are just stretched so much, they don't have enough time to be kids," notes Texas teacher Linda DeMino Duffy. "They're on sports teams, they're taking piano lessons—but in actuality, we're creating an environment where someone is always stimulating them. They don't know how to be by themselves.

"I think the best thing you can do for your child is just to give them experiences. Let them experience life. Don't go overboard. Just live your life, but be open to doing different things."

garden together. This list should not be elaborate or detailed, and it is not meant to impress the neighbors or make sure your child gets into a good college. These are simply the "extras" of your schedule, things that you'd really enjoy doing if only you could find the time. Now you can look for the time.

Even if you don't plan to have a written schedule posted in your home, it's still best to jot this all down on a sheet of paper. Try writing approximate times by each, and seeing how long things take. Does it all fit? Looking at what you're doing, do your days feel both comfortable and valuable to you? Writing this down forces you to set priorities and identify periods during the day or week that are too busy and need to be reexamined.

If you'd like to just keep this in a notebook and take a look at it every so often, that is fine. Revisiting it occasionally will help you see if you're on track for living the life you value. You can still discuss your day's plans with your child each morning, without referring to a written schedule.

If you create a written schedule that you plan to review daily with your child and that she can consult, here are some ways schedules work in the classroom and some fun ways to create them at home.

How Schedules Are Used in the Classroom and at Home

In Mrs. Rice's classroom, her schedule is posted near the group meeting area, where the class can discuss it each morning and refer to it throughout the day. The activities are written, and include a simple line drawing to signal the activity (for example, the word "Reading" has a drawing of a book beside it).

Her classroom schedule remains relatively the same each day, except when there's a special class, guest speaker, or field trip. Then she writes a separate message explaining the changes in the day, with the special event written in at its appropriate spot. The class discusses this when they go over the schedule.

Her students rely on the schedule as a visual cue to understand how the day will unfold. The students often refer to it individually—for instance, a student may walk up to the schedule and count how many activities are left before recess or lunch.

Mrs. Rice also uses the schedule to give her students a chance to plan their time and make decisions about how to use their time. If the students are particularly excited about a reading lesson and she devotes extra time to that, she and the students might discuss during snack time how they're going to work in their math lesson.

At home, your schedule might be as detailed as the one Mrs. Rice uses in her classroom; for example, you might use poster board or a dry-erase board to list all of the day's activities and post it in a common family area. Or it could be more general:

Wake-up time and breakfast
Playtime and jobs
Lunch
Outside playtime
Dinner
Quiet activities, bedtime routine

You could even eliminate the obvious things—waking up and eating—and just jot down the things that are different about each day, so everyone has a visual reminder of what to expect.

Note what is *not* included in these schedules. You are making sure your child has time to play outside, not scheduling 5 minutes to play hopscotch, then 15 minutes to search for and classify bugs, followed by 10 minutes to write letters and numbers in chalk on the sidewalk.

Remember that schedules are not a way to control or dictate exactly what your child does when, but simply a tool to provide a structure for your days.

Developing Routines or Procedures

Schedules define the *what* and *when* of your days—what needs to happen and when? Routines provide the *how*. How do we get ready for bed at night? We take a bath, put on our pajamas, drink some milk, go to the bathroom, brush our teeth, and read a story. That is our bedtime routine. A routine basically is a rhythm for doing the same things in essentially the same way each time. It allows you to do things simply and automatically, and provides important cues for your child about what comes next.

You do not have to develop a routine in the same way you establish a schedule. It can fall into place more naturally. But you do need to think about it—what parts of your day would benefit from having a routine, or expected, way of handling them? Are the routines you have now working?

In Illinois, teacher Randy Heite has discovered he's been able to replace almost all of his classroom rules with well-planned and carefully practiced routines or procedures.

For instance, when students first visit his classroom before the start of the school year, he introduces them to the "lunch procedure," because he's learned that it's one thing almost every incoming kindergartner worries about. He shows them exactly where their names are going to be on laminated strips of paper, and how to take a ticket showing whether they have a lunch from home or want to buy lunch. He lets them practice attaching the ticket to the appropriate basket, as they'll do each morning of the school year.

Mr. Heite spends a good deal of the first two or three weeks of the school year simply introducing the students to classroom procedures like these. He does this because he realized early in his teaching career that many of the apparent behavior problems he faced each day were actually problems with children understanding and following the classroom procedures.

"Once I started to identify the things my kids struggled with in my classroom, I was really able to identify and see what caused the most confusion. And it became obvious to me that it was really my fault—I didn't have the right procedure set up," he explains.

"So I went through my day, asking what can I do? What changes can I make as their teacher to make sure I set up their environment and procedures for them, so they know what to do?"

While Mr. Heite notes he definitely *had* procedures for things like checking in for lunch and handling the morning meeting before, he never really sat down with the kids and examined the procedures from their vantage point.

He now has procedures in place for just about every task in his classroom, including taking care of the class animals. "A child might say to me, 'Oh, Mr. Heite, I'm supposed to take care of Maxie the turtle this week!' And I'll say: 'Have you ever done it before, do you know the procedure?' I talk about it that way, as a procedure: 'Here's how you get his food. Here's how you open his cage.'"

And Mr. Heite notes: "The key is spending the time to really establish that routine or procedure. A lot of times in early childhood, people introduce something and expect the kids to remember it. But the truth is, you have to practice."

Or as Kentucky teacher Patrice McCrary explains: "Procedures are critical in a classroom. But they go smoothly only after a great deal of practice. You need to get your procedures *firmly* in place in order to save time."

At home, you might have a routine or a procedure for getting dressed in the morning, getting out the door, getting ready for mealtime, or getting to bed. Practice this with your child so she knows what is expected. Try it yourself, preferably from your child's level, to be certain it works and makes sense. Note any areas that tend to cause trouble, and be willing to adapt the procedure if needed (but don't be *too* ready to change—remember, procedures require plenty of practice before they work smoothly).

Using Calendars Effectively

In addition to daily schedules, it's helpful to have a way to keep track of what's coming up next week and next month—a calendar. Calendars are most effective if they're in a spot accessible to everyone in the family. This allows even young children to see what's coming up.

A simply drawn picture or sticker placed next to a day's event can cue your child into the day's events. "How many days until my birthday?" Or "How long until Grandma visits?" can be answered with: "Check the family calendar for a picture of a cake." Or "Look at the calendar for the picture of Grandma."

Good early childhood teachers love using calendars in the classroom because they provide such a great introduction to important premath and prereading skills.

In Hawaii, teacher Pauline Jacroux uses a large wall calendar that has three squares along each side. At calendar time each day, the "calendar monitor" points out each element of the date, "Today is Monday, February 20, 2007."

Along one side of the calendar, the first box is for the child to draw a picture to record the weather—for instance, sunny or rainy. In the next box, she records whether it is a windy day, based upon a report from a classmate who steps out the classroom door with a windsock. In the third box, she records the temperature, using a thermometer outside the classroom door.

Along the other side of the calendar, one of the boxes is used to record what day of school it is, as the children celebrate the 100th day of school. The next box is unique to Mrs. Jacroux's Hawaii classroom—it is used to record whether the children see a bird called the Golden Plether, which arrives in August to take up residence outside the classroom each year before migrating to Alaska each April. The bottom box is used to record the phase of the moon.

Your calendar at home can be just as detailed, or simple. But by using a calendar, you're teaching your child about numbers, days of the week, and the concepts of today, tomorrow, and yesterday. You're also teaching counting, and helping him to recognize letters and words. You're also teaching the basics of:

- Measurement, if you compare the elements of time. ("How many days are between Sue's birthday and Sally's?")
- Problem solving and classifying, if you try to figure out what the weather might be like during a given month.
- Graphing, if you use symbols such as a sunshine, raindrops, or snow to track the weather each day.

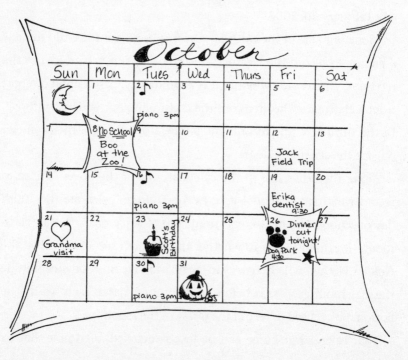

CARD CLIP

AGES: 3–5

Materials: Index cards, small clothespins, 24-inch piece of wide ribbon, markers

Preparation: With your child, draw a picture for each of the day's important events on the index cards. Use the clothespins to attach the cards to the length of ribbon. Hang the ribbon on a wall or door so that your child can reach the cards.

What to Do: When your child completes an activity, he can take off the corresponding index card. The card can be put into a nearby box, basket, or envelope to be used another day. Each evening, replace the cards using the appropriate ones for the next day's activities.

NOTEBOOK SCHEDULE

AGES: 4–6

Materials: Paper, markers, three-ring binder, page protectors

Preparation: With your child, draw a picture for each of the day's important events on individual sheets of paper. Put the papers into page protectors.

What to Do: Pick the sheets that show the day's appropriate activities, then arrange them in order in the three-ring binder. Your child can then refer to the notebook throughout the day, and you can easily change parts of the schedule from day to day.

SCHEDULE BOARD GAME

AGES: 3–6

Materials: Paper, markers, checkers or coins to use as game tokens

Preparation: With your child, draw a simple game board path of boxes. Draw simple pictures along the path of the things your child needs to do in the morning, afternoon, or evening.

What to Do: Have your child move his game piece every time he completes an activity on the schedule, until he "wins" by reaching the end of the path.

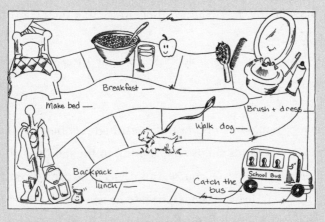

Morning Schedule

Assigning Tasks or Household Jobs

Early childhood classrooms have jobs posted for the students—plant waterer, line leader, calendar helper, paper collector. This is because jobs give children a chance to take on some responsibility and ownership in the classroom, and keep the students from expecting the teacher to do everything for them.

At home, in addition to cleaning up her toys when she's done playing or putting away her crayons when she's done coloring, your child should have a few jobs that show her she is a contributing and important member of the family. Helping gives your child a sense of growing up and an understanding that belonging to a group—a family, a classroom, or a workplace—means making some contributions rather than simply taking. It also allows them to see that their contributions are valued.

When assigning household tasks to your three- to six-year-old, remember:

- The job should be important or meaningful enough so that your child understands she is contributing to the family, rather than simply filling time. Of course, this needs to be considered on your child's level. He likely values the jobs he sees you doing—bringing in the mail, emptying the dishwasher, dusting the furniture, even sorting the laundry.

- You should not hover or constantly correct your child's work. Teach your child how to do the job. Practice until she can do it on her own. Then leave her to do it. Do not follow her around fixing her "mistakes." Allow her to do the work, and experience the sense of pride and accomplishment that follows. If you need to reteach an aspect of the job, do so in a helpful and respectful way. Remember that what starts slowly today will become routine in time.

Some Appropriate Jobs for Three- to Six-Year-Olds

- Sweeping the front steps or floor, with a child-sized broom.
- Putting dirty clothes into a laundry basket or hamper.
- Sorting clean socks.
- Watering the plants.
- Putting clean laundry into drawers.
- Helping to put away groceries.
- Pulling weeds from the garden.
- Raking leaves, with a child-sized rake.
- Making the beds.
- Helping to feed the pets.
- Putting clean spoons and forks into the silverware drawer.
- Getting the newspaper or mail (with parent watching).
- Using a feather duster or dry-dusting wipe on the furniture.
- Loading and unloading unbreakable items in the dishwasher.
- Setting the table (breakable dishes should be brought to the table by a parent).

In addition, your child should begin taking more responsibility for caring for herself—learning to put on her own clothes, wipe up her own spills, and put her own trash in the garbage. Many early childhood teachers refuse to do anything for a child that he could do for himself.

In the words of Mrs. Jacroux from Hawaii: "I do not lean down and pick up pencils off the floor. Things that they can do for themselves, let them do. Plan extra time if you need to. It may take longer for them to do it. But don't do for them what they can do for themselves. That just undermines them."

GETTING YOUR DUCKS IN A ROW

AGES: 3–4

Materials: Rubber ducks; permanent marker; bathtub, sink, or basin

Preparation: On the bottom of each duck, write a job for your child to do.

What to Do: Float the ducks in the bathroom sink or bin of water. Let your child pick a duck (or catch one in a net) and do the job. Best of all, your child may want to choose more jobs once the first is done!

Variation: Write jobs on slips of paper and put them into a jar or wide plastic cup. Let your child choose a few each day to complete.

JOB CUBE

AGES: 4–6

Materials: Square tissue box, paper, markers

Preparation: Cover tissue box with paper. On each side, write a job that your child can do. Determine how many rolls of the "job cube" your child will need to do for the day.

What to Do: Have your child roll the "job cube" and complete whatever job it lands on. If it lands on a job that is already completed, your child chooses a silly action everyone must do (squawk like a chicken, do a hula dance, run in place, etc.). The cube can then be rolled until an uncompleted job comes up.

FLOWER POWER

AGES: 4–5

Materials: Construction paper, scissors, markers, double-sided tape or small cut strips of tape, glue, envelope or small container

Preparation: Cut out a flower center, stem, leaves, and six to eight flower petals from construction paper. On the center of the flower write "My Jobs." On each petal, write a job that is part of your child's daily job list. (You could also draw a simple picture.) Glue the flower center to a piece of paper. Add the stem and leaves. On the back of each petal, attach double-sided tape. Hang the paper with the flower center on a door or wall at your child's level. Put the petals into an envelope or container nearby.

What to Do: Have your child pick a petal and do the job listed on it. When the job is done, attach the petal around the center of the flower. When all jobs are done, the flower will be complete.

TREASURE MAP

AGES: 4–6

Materials: Paper, markers

Preparation: Draw a simple map with pictures leading your child through the day's jobs. End with a fun activity you can do together, such as baking cookies, playing a game, or going for a walk together.

What to Do: Give your child the treasure map to follow, and do the fun activity together once all the jobs are successfully completed.

Variation: End at a location where you've hidden a decorated shoe box or jewelry box with a small "treasure," such as stickers or coupons for fun activities.

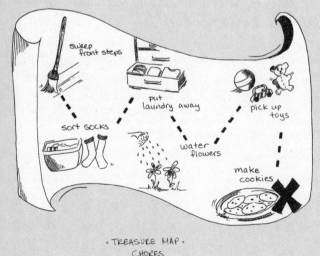

= TREASURE MAP =
CHORES

6

MAKING AND USING RULES CREATIVELY

A Handful of Rules Can Do the Job

If there's one rule good teachers know about making rules for young children, it's to make as few of them as possible. Most of the best early childhood classrooms have perhaps three or four rules governing student behavior, and some teachers would argue even that is too many.

How is this possible? How can a teacher safely run a classroom—or a parent a home—with only a handful of rules?

It happens partly because of the steps we discussed in the two previous chapters: organizing space and structuring time. You might not need to make a rule saying, "All toys must be put away before bedtime," if you've already established a simple before-bed routine that includes picking up toys, and you've set up a specific and accessible place to put the toys.

And it happens if your rules are well-formed and meaningful. The best and most useful rules focus on the few things that tend to cause the most trouble. They're formed so that they can be applied consistently, and can be used in (or adapted to) many situations.

A good set of rules will increase your child's sense of safety or security. Rules can give her a better sense of how to behave within a community, and ultimately make your lives more peaceful and cooperative. The tricky parts, which we'll outline in more detail throughout this chapter, are:

- Deciding how to form your household rules.
- Deciding how you'll enforce them—or making a plan for what to do when things go wrong.
- Deciding whether to reward your child for "good" behavior.

If You Have More Than One Child

Be sure to include them all when creating and explaining the rules. Household rules should apply to everyone. But when enforcing the rules, it's important to keep each child's own personality and temperament in mind. If one child needs firmer instructions, it's okay to provide them for that child, even if the other responds better to gentle reminders.

How Should Your Rules Be Formed?

In forming rules for your household, you should consider your own parenting style and the needs of your home. You can make your rules quite specific, or more general. Specific rules—"Always say *please* when you ask for something and *thank you* when you're given something"— clearly tell your child what is expected. It is obvious whether the rule is being followed or being broken. It teaches something important that the child can use at home, at school, or at a friend's house. And the rule stays the same no matter how tired you are or what kind of mood you're in.

However, specific rules sometimes are limited—the one above, for example, doesn't teach your child about good manners in general. A general rule ("Use good manners," or even, "Respect others") is more adaptable, but you need to take the time to explain what the rule means. While some would argue that general rules are too vague to be truly meaningful to a young child, many good early childhood teachers see them as an opportunity to integrate lessons about the "rules" throughout the day, guiding the children to true life lessons.

How do you know what sort of rules your household needs? It depends upon what issues you are trying to resolve and who you are as a parent—or how you plan to enforce the rules.

If you're dealing with a specific behavior problem, you might be best framing the rule to that problem. For instance, in Mrs. Rice's kindergarten classroom, she knows exactly what issues and activities during the day cause the most trouble. She has designed her classroom rules around those. Her rules are:

- Try to follow directions the first time they're given.
- Try to raise your hand before speaking out loud.
- Respect the personal space of those around you.
- Put all things back where you found them.

Her rules are quite specific, yet adaptable to a variety of situations she might face in her classroom. It is obvious when a rule is being broken, and easy for her to point out what the rule says and how the child can adjust her behavior. Mrs. Rice's rules also cover her day's problem areas nicely, and teach students the skills they need to succeed and get along in the classroom. (She did have to adapt the third rule, which originally said, Respect the personal space of your friends, when one student tried to argue that the child he was bothering was not a friend!)

You may decide to craft specific rules to regulate behavior at mealtime, teach siblings how to resolve disputes without pushing or hitting, or help your child get through bathtime and bedtime peacefully. Notice that you could also tackle the mealtime and bedtime issues by establishing clear routines or procedures at these times. However, even with specific routines in place, a reminder in the form of a rule could help with a trouble area. While kindergarten teacher Randy Heite has replaced almost all of his rules with procedures (see Chapter 5), he still reminds his students about the proper behavior when walking down the hallway with this rule: "No touching, no talking, just walking."

In Maryland, award-winning teacher Dara Feldman wanted to keep order in her classroom while focusing on greater life lessons. So she approached rules in her kindergarten class in Garrett Park with guiding principles. Mrs. Feldman, who was recognized as a national Disney Teacher Award honoree in 2005, crafted a classroom pledge, which her students brought home and signed with their parents. It read: "We will be peaceful with our words and actions. We will be gentle with people and things. We will be enthusiastic learners and always try our best."

Notice how nicely this, too, addresses problem areas and gives Mrs. Feldman a specific rule to point to when common kindergarten troubles erupt. Her students helped write the pledge, and at that time they talked specifically about what each item meant. They also drew pictures to illustrate the items. And she provided gentle reminders when things went wrong.

This is important to remember at home as well. You need to explain the rules to your child. It's extremely helpful to explain *why* your rules are important. In her classroom, Pauline Jacroux allows her students to help form the rules, brainstorming for ideas and narrowing them down to the most important three or four.

"And we always discuss the reasons for having rules: to keep everyone safe, to make sure everyone is treated with respect," she notes.

In considering your own style and ability to provide consistency and direction, it's helpful to know that, in some ways, specific directions are the easiest to enforce, because it's clear when they're broken and what needs to be done to correct the behavior. The rule does most of the work for you.

If you choose to establish a general set of guidelines, you need to be the one to provide that consistency and direction. Make sure your child knows what is expected, and don't misuse the rule by changing the definition to suit your needs from day to day. Know that it might take more time to convey your meaning, so correct gently and with a clear explanation of how the behavior breaks the rule.

Some other questions early childhood teachers consider when crafting their classroom rules include:

Should the rules be worded as Do's or Don'ts?

Teachers generally agree that your rules should state what you *want* to happen, not the behavior you're trying to avoid. So you wouldn't establish a rule that said: "Don't leave your toys lying on the floor," but instead one that said: "Put your toys away when you're finished playing." There are several reasons for this, but the primary one is that young children have a difficult time flipping the *Don't* into a *Do*. They may understand you don't want the toys on the floor, but that doesn't necessarily help them figure out what to do.

However, there are some rules that are just tough to turn around—especially since rules are most effective when they're clear and understandable. If I want a rule that keeps my kids from running in the house, my rule might simply be: "No running in the house." A good teacher might argue that I need to phrase this rule as a positive—what should the children do instead of running? Perhaps it could be: "Only walking in the house." But that's not what I mean. I don't mind occasional skipping, or rolling, or crawling in the house. I just don't want running. Maybe something like: "Move respectfully through the house." But to me, this is confusing and doesn't say what I mean. Patrice McCrary in Kentucky cleverly tackled this one with: "Speed limit: Walking." I may borrow that.

But in the meantime, know that if you find you need a *Don't* rule, it's okay—and certainly better than a rule that doesn't say what you mean. The most important thing is that your rules are clear and understandable. And remember that even though the rule itself may be a *Don't,* when you correct, you need to give clear directions for what you want to happen. "Slow down! Walk down the hallway, please."

Should the rules be written down and posted?

Most early childhood teachers have the class rules posted somewhere in the classroom. This way, they can refer to them throughout the day as needed, and the children have a clear and visible reminder of what is expected.

Many parents are resistant to posting rules in their homes, and I can certainly understand this. However, my thinking on this shifted a bit one day while visiting a resort town with some friends. As we walked down the town's main street, lined with shops and restaurants, we passed a diner that had a sign posted on the front door: "Restrooms are for customers only." And I realized: Posted rules do their job.

You could choose to post the rules only if you are tackling a specific behavior and feel your child needs that visible reminder. Or as an alternative to posting the rules on the refrigerator or a wall, you could develop a "rule book" that you and your child make together, illustrating each rule. Keep it in an accessible place, and refer to it as needed.

When the Rules Are Broken: Balancing Love and Authority

Once you've established your rules, you need to think about how you're going to implement them—or what will happen when rules are broken. For good early childhood teachers, this discussion is almost always framed in the context of *guidance* or *redirection,* or perhaps *consequences*, rather than *punishment*. That's because their goal is to teach their young students about getting along in a community—to learn they are capable of controlling their own behavior and of fixing their mistakes. In helping your child discover this at home, you should try to balance two things:

- Your child should know she can trust you, that you are someone who loves her and keeps her safe.
- Your child should know that you're comfortable taking charge—you're not afraid of or unwilling to accept your own authority as a parent.

Both of these principles can be summed up this way: You want to impart a sense that you and your child are on the same team. You, of course, would be considered the leader or coach of that team. But you are not out to win some sort of battle against your child. You are not on opposing teams. You are guiding her toward the skills she needs to succeed, and you're doing this out of a sense of love and support.

Accepting Your Authority as a Parent

What does this mean in day-to-day life?

First, effective teachers accept the authority they have as teachers. They know they are in charge, and they have a plan. They are prepared.

At home, you need to accept your authority as a parent. And you need to think about your plan—what will you do if things don't go smoothly? You need some tools for when trouble starts to erupt. Teacher Jackie Cooke in Oregon notes that in the early stages of misbehavior, any of these techniques could bring things back under control: shaking your head, standing in close proximity to the child, or quietly pulling a child aside and asking, "What rule are you having trouble following?"

Mrs. Jacroux simply asks: "Are you doing the right thing?"

"For some reason, they never argue with that simple concept," she says. "After that, just wide eyes, or 'stink eye' as we call it in Hawaii, may shape them up."

But if things do continue spiraling out of control—your child is refusing to hear your directions, or acting in a manner that is unsafe to him or others—do not simply throw up your hands or give up in frustration. Do not complain: "You never listen to me!" or "I don't know what to do with you!" Remember, like an effective teacher, that you are the adult. Your first job is to get a handle on the situation. You may need to pretend you are in control, even if you fear you are not. In a firm voice, you can use one of these phrases:

"Stop right now!"
"Absolutely not!"
"Enough!"
"Not a chance!"

In other words, immediately stop the activity and bring the situation back under adult control. Make sure your tone of voice and facial expression convey the same message—don't smile gently or talk hesitantly. Give clear directions that say what you want to happen: And follow through until your child complies—remaining calm, firm, and in control.

"When the class is 'losing control,' my first response is to get their attention *without* trying to 'shout them out,'" explains Mrs. Jacroux.

"Do whatever it takes. I use several techniques depending upon the circumstances: turn out the lights, blow a train whistle—yes, I have one!

"Once I turned out the lights, closed the doors, and shut the window louvers, so that I was stumbling around in the dark until my eyes adjusted. We sat in silence for a while before I asked them what was happening.

"Once you have their attention, you speak in a quieter voice than usual so they really have to listen to you. Then choose the appropriate message, give it logically and with humor, if possible, and definitely with love and concern for them."

And When Your Child Is Just Not Listening?

The truth is, this can be difficult in real life. Your child is not listening to you. You know you need to follow through, but how? When your child just is not listening, how do you stay in control?

The key to answering this question is to remember that you are the adult. It is your job to keep your child safe. You are in charge. Hang on to that feeling of being in charge, or in control. It will help you actually stay in control—of the situation and your own emotions.

Remember, when you are giving your child directions that you expect her to follow, do not ask permission: "I want you to go brush your teeth, okay?" Similarly, do not get drawn into a debate about why your child should do what you're directing. If your child does not listen, calmly and firmly repeat your direction. "It's time to brush your teeth." Get down on the child's level and make eye contact.

If your direction is still ignored, assume it was simply misunderstood and say it again, perhaps phrasing it another way. "Go into the bathroom and get your toothbrush so you can brush your teeth."

Resist the urge to up the ante by yelling or responding with a "stronger" or more escalated response ("You'd better be in the bathroom brushing your teeth by the time I count to three or you're going into time-out!") This makes you look weak and out of control, and it appears to give the child a choice: "Listen to me, or..." You are not giving your child a choice of whether to listen to your directions or accept a punishment. You want your directions followed. You might want to think of this as the "broken-record technique," because you are restating your instructions until they're followed.

Another technique that might help if your child is still refusing to follow your directions and you're starting to feel yourself getting frustrated: Change the direction from a *go* command: "Go brush your teeth right now!" to a *come* direction. "Come with me. We need to brush your teeth." The word "come" can steer you away from escalating the confrontation and toward cooperation, while still ensuring your directions are followed and you remain in control. (And it gives you the useful alternative of then taking your child by the hand or gently picking her up and bringing her with you to the bathroom to brush her teeth.)

Another alternative, especially useful if your child has lost control of her emotions during the battle, is to temporarily change direction and give her a related task she can successfully complete. "Hand me that tissue box on the table. Thank you. Let's wipe your eyes so you feel a little better. Okay, now let's go get your teeth brushed, so we can read a story before bed."

Don't Be Afraid to Ask for Help

As teacher Linda DeMino Duffy reminds us, "I think it is very important that a teacher believes she has authority, but it is also important that she realizes that to ask for assistance from another adult is not an indication that she does not have control of her students."

In other words, it's okay to ask for help. The key is: You still need to remain calm and in control, and it's best to have a plan. "Different kids need different things, and sometimes a different adult with a different approach or personality can make a difference in defusing a situation," Mrs. Duffy explains.

She uses the example of a child who is misbehaving and refusing to go to the library. She might signal a different adult—another teacher, the librarian, a coach, or even the custodian—to walk by that child and chat with him, which could be enough to divert the child's attention or change his frame of mind.

"By doing these things, you could never diminish your 'authority' over the children, because they will understand and appreciate that their environment has order and a plan," she notes.

Mrs. Rice once had a student who became unbudgeable whenever something did not go her way. "She would roll on to her stomach, draw in her knees, and refuse to talk, move, look up, or listen," Mrs. Rice recalls, even if the class was walking down a crowded hallway and other students had to step around or over her.

None of Mrs. Rice's usual tricks worked. When the girl fell into tantrum position and refused to leave the room during a fire drill, Mrs. Rice had to admit she needed help. So she made a plan. When the girl began a tantrum, Mrs. Rice would send a note to another adult, and the person would come into her classroom and simply remain with the girl, without talking, until the tantrum passed.

This continued until one day the girl did not get a doll she wanted and dropped into her tantrum position. Mrs. Rice went to her desk to get her note. "From her curled-up position, I heard a muffled, 'Don't send it, teacher.' And she got up and went to play."

As Mrs. Rice notes: "I wasn't incompetent, ineffective, or doing anything wrong—I simply needed to ask for help."

Providing Guidance or Redirection

Once the situation is back in your control, you can move on to your primary goal: providing guidance or redirection. First, you need to make sure everyone—including you—is in control of his or her emotions and ready to move on. If the situation has escalated to the point where you or your child is feeling overly emotional, but everyone is safe and the situation is under your control, you could choose to simply redirect to another activity.

For instance, kindergarten teacher Susie Haas-Kane in California notes that virtually no child in this age group could resist a good story.

"I recommend to younger teachers, if they have a moment where the kids are not listening, to stop everything. Then say: 'Let's go to the rug and read a story.' Get the kids tuned in to you again. Get control, and bring yourself back down a little."

At home, you could similarly shift gears and get your child back into a "listening" frame of mind by pulling out a good book to read to her.

Otherwise, you could choose to have a short discussion: "This is not working. No one will be allowed to play until we all understand the rules. What can we do now to make this work?"

This is one format good teachers use for one-on-one discussions, or "guidance talks," when rules have been broken or a situation has spiraled out of control:

1. Bring the situation back under adult control.
2. Explain what went wrong—what rule or principle was broken? ("Jack, you pushed Lucy down. We take care of each other in this house.")
3. Express how everyone involved may have felt. ("You were frustrated she took your toy. But when you pushed her, that hurt her.")
4. Give a clear alternative to what to do next time. ("You can tell her you were still using that toy.")
5. Give the child a chance to make it right. ("Let's go get the boo-boo bunny to hold on her knee so it feels better.")

Another technique to defuse the situation once it's back under your control is by asking your child to do a "rewind," giving him another chance to start from scratch and do it right. In Mrs. Jacroux's Hawaii classroom, she explains: "If I say, 'I want you to come in the classroom quietly,' and they come in and immediately start running around, you say: 'I'm sorry, go back outside and try it again.' Then you always tell them what gains they made: 'That was much better. You did this and this and this. You still need to work on this, so let's try it one more time.'"

At home, this technique is especially useful if no other child was hurt or involved with the incident. ("We take care of our things in this house. Don't throw your toys. Let's try that again, and you can show me how to put toys down gently.")

Quiet Time Versus Time-Out

When a child misbehaves, parents and teachers alike often rely upon a "time-out" to redirect the child's behavior. However, some early childhood teachers feel the concept of "time-out" has become overused and punitive. In their classrooms, it is instead framed as a "quiet time," or a break needed to relax, refocus, and settle. It's used most commonly when a child is having a temper tantrum or physical outburst.

Before a "quiet time," a child might be approached gently with the words "You could use a quiet time to relax." If the child is having a full-blown tantrum or is physically aggressive, it is equally important to help the child "save face" with his peers, who have probably stopped all activities to watch, thus increasing the frustration and embarrassment of the angry child. You might say, "It's time to move away from this place. You need some time for yourself." In this way, the child's initial needs are met (attention), the adult's needs are met (restoring order), and they can now move to problem solving or redirection.

The next step is to help the child express his anger or frustration, then focus on what can be an alternate response the next time it occurs. The child may draw in a quiet time journal, a notebook provided at the quiet time area. In the journal, the child is free to draw any type of picture or face that reflects how he is feeling. After this drawing, the child is asked to draw what could be done next time. This approach allows the adult to attend to the needs of the others before going back to the child taking a quiet time.

Mrs. Haas recommends simply removing the child from the situation for a few moments.

"Punishment, yelling, it's just going to cause havoc," she says. "Instead, say, 'I need you to go sit down for two minutes'—that calm, that simple. It immediately helps the situation."

Some Reminders

As you provide corrections and redirection:

- Try not to say something that simply isn't true, for example, "We don't hit our sister!" when he just hit his sister. This is confusing, and obviously untrue. As South Carolina teacher Stephanie Seay notes: "If we have to say, 'We don't hit others,' we're wrong because obviously the hitting has already taken place." Instead, clearly say what you mean: "Don't hit your sister! You hurt her!"

- Do your best to give your child the tools he needs to solve the problem in a better way, clearly explaining an alternative: "Tell her you had the ball first and you're still playing with it." Again turning to Mrs. Seay: "We're so good at pointing out the wrong behavior. 'Here's what you can do instead'—that's the piece that's often missing."
- Finally, look for a way for your child to make it right, or fix his mistakes: "Let's go get some ice for her to hold on her arm."

This last point is very important, as your ultimate goal isn't necessarily to punish your child for making mistakes, but to help him fix the mistakes he makes and learn how to avoid them in the future.

Remember that the best teachers approach conflict knowing they want to be the child's ally, not her opponent. You can turn every incident into a confrontation or a battle of wills, or you can remain consistent, in control, and teach your child how to manage her emotions and resolve conflict. We'll talk much more about this in the next chapter, but first, let's take a quick look at the other side of the coin: whether to provide rewards when the rules are followed.

To Reward or Not to Reward?

Early childhood teachers sometimes use a simple reward system for good behavior. Mrs. Haas, for example, gives out "Wow tickets" in her California kindergarten classroom. A "Wow ticket" is nothing more than a strip of colored construction paper.

(When a child gets a Wow ticket, she must write her name on it, so this is one of Mrs. Haas's classroom tricks for getting her students to practice writing their names.)

All the Wow tickets go into a box, and Mrs. Haas pulls out about five a week for students to pick a small reward (though she doesn't really read the name on the ticket, instead manipulating it so every child eventually gets a trip to the treasure box).

While Mrs. Rice doesn't offer individual rewards, she does use a class marble jar—when all the students complete cleanup on time or get themselves quickly on task for a project, she drops a marble or two into the jar, explaining what the class did to earn it. When the marble jar is full, the class gets to vote on a class reward: perhaps they can bring a book in to share before naptime, or watch an appropriate video together, or have a special show-and-tell day.

Similarly, Mrs. Cooke's students in Oregon earn points they can trade as a class for rewards such as an extra recess or a pretend slumber party.

Parents can transfer these reward systems to home, but need to keep some guidelines in mind so the rewards don't instead become bribes. The key is to name and recognize good behavior, so the child can learn to recognize it. The danger is establishing a system where the child becomes motivated by the reward itself.

Good early childhood teachers are wary of an essential danger in rewards: Children can become too attached to the reward. For instance, they might learn to rely on generous praise or a cheerful sticker to judge whether they did something well, rather than learning how to evaluate this for themselves. Or they might decide good behavior isn't worthwhile on its own, but only worth the effort if the reward is good enough.

Frequent rewards actually diminish a child's natural inclination to learn how to master a task for its own sake. Children have a great natural reward system, which allows them to work hard at doing things simply because they're interested. With an external reward system, they can begin to act solely for the reward, not the internal satisfaction of learning something new or doing something well.

This means that rewards should be small, used sparingly, and generally reserved for tasks that offer little reward of their own—for instance, you shouldn't offer a reward for learning something new, but you might offer one for changing a troublesome behavior or following through completely on a task that would otherwise become tedious.

If you're looking for rewards to offer at home, consider choices based on the classroom models, such as:

- A picnic at the park.
- A slumber party with you and your children.
- A family movie night.
- A game night where everyone teaches the others their favorite game.
- A "crazy clothes" day, when you all wear odd or mismatched clothes.

When offering rewards, remember not to mistakenly offer a bribe. A bribe puts the child in control, while a reward is something you control. This would be a bribe: "If you stay quiet while I'm putting your baby sister down for a nap, I'll give you a new coloring book." This gives the child a choice of whether to behave in the way you'd simply expect and allows her to decide if the reward of a new coloring book is "enough" for her to behave.

To give rewards effectively, you should simply state your expectations: "I'll need you to be quiet while I put your sister down for a nap. Then when she's sleeping, you and I can color together."

You could also choose to use a sticker to mark each time she is able to remain quiet during naptime, and offer a small reward once she accumulates a certain amount of stickers. Mrs. Haas notes that the Wow tickets work so well in part because young children just love the word "ticket." So you might offer tickets of your own, perhaps having your child collect a certain number of tickets and then being allowed to turn them in for a reward.

In Mrs. Seay's classroom in South Carolina, she shies away from rewards altogether, trying to teach her students to evaluate their own work and behavior rather than relying on praise or rewards from her. Similarly, Texas teacher Mrs. Duffy encourages her students to feel proud of themselves for doing their best.

"When a child does something nice or does good work, I think it is important to get them to understand that they should feel good about what they have done and not rely on being rewarded by an adult," she says. "Some kids will do anything to be praised, and in the beginning I will praise them, but I also begin to ask them questions like: 'How did it make you feel when you...' or 'Why did you do such nice work? Does it make you feel proud to do your best? You should be proud of yourself!'

"I want them to find their inner voice that helps make them feel good about the choices they make," she explains. "I don't just want them to rely on my praise, because they will not always get praised by a teacher, parent, or future boss."

While she hesitates to reward children for their work, Mrs. Duffy gives her students "warm fuzzies" when they do something nice for someone else. The "warm fuzzies" are different-sized and multicolored pompoms balls that you can buy at a craft store. The kids have a warm fuzzy container at home that they can collect them in.

Mrs. Seay similarly uses a beaded satin box as a "kindness box." When she notices someone displaying kind behavior, such as helping a classmate clean up spilled paint, she jots a note recognizing that and drops it into the box. Children can similarly recognize a classmate, drawing a picture of a kind act they witnessed and dropping it into the box.

"That's the extent of the reward," Mrs. Seay explains, "just that simple acknowledgment."

Adapting a Native American tradition she learned of in a teacher workshop, Mrs. Seay also has a "Jar of Seed" she uses, scooping birdseed into the jar when she observes kind or helpful behavior. When the jar is full, the class goes outside and scatters the seed for the birds. You could easily do the same at home.

"The message we discuss is: When acts of kindness come to us, we acknowledge or record that in some way, and then return that kindness to someone else," she says.

7

RESOLVING CONFLICTS AND RESPONDING TO STRONG EMOTIONS

Take about two dozen young children, mix them together in a class-room, and a few things are bound to happen during the course of any day. Someone will certainly cry. A few children will argue passionately over a toy or a friend. And at least several students will rush to their teacher with complaints about others, looking for her to intervene.

How does a good early childhood teacher do it? How does she cope with all the emotion, fighting, and drama? How does she manage to get any *teaching* done in the midst of it? And how can you take what she knows and apply it to home, where you also certainly face a few tears, some disputes, and plenty of drama?

The truth is that an effective early childhood teacher spends a good chunk of her day helping her young students learn to manage their emotions and resolve conflicts on their own. Ultimately, she resists any urge to jump in and solve her students' problems for them, instead giving them the skills and tools to figure out solutions themselves.

By learning her techniques, you can help your child learn ways to soothe herself when things go wrong, and begin to find ways to solve problems and resolve conflict on her own. But first, it's important to help your child:

- Learn to recognize and name emotions—to know what it looks and sounds like to be happy, sad, frustrated, hopeful, disappointed, excited, surprised, or hurt.
- Understand that feelings change—a feeling is a temporary response, and it does not last forever.
- Learn the difference between feelings and actions—in other words, to begin to appreciate that while all of her feelings are okay, it's up to her to decide the best response to those feelings.

Learning to Recognize and Name Emotions

Children can learn to recognize and name emotions starting by age two. To help your child do this, start by simply naming and explaining your own feelings during the course of the day: "I'm so excited we're going to the playground today! It should be a lot of fun," or "I was disappointed when I had to work late, because I was really looking forward to being home in time for dinner."

Before moving on to helping your child recognize and name his own feelings, you first should be sure he has a basic grasp of emotions. Early childhood teachers sometimes call this "building a feelings' vocabulary," and you can use the activities that follow to do this.

Once your child seems to have a good understanding of feelings in general, you could talk about your child's own emotions. When early childhood teachers do this in the classroom, they try to avoid simply *telling* a child what she feels. (Remember, you're not trying to control or change her feelings, but just to occasionally reflect them back to her.) Similarly at home, rather than saying: "You're disappointed," or "You feel sad," you could begin: "It looks like you feel..." or "I wonder if you feel..." Rather than reassuring with the words: "There's no reason to be so sad," simply reflect the feeling: "You look very sad."

SING A FEELINGS SONG

AGES: 3–4

Materials: None.

Preparation: None.

What to Do: Sing a song you and your child know well using different emotions. Use a song like "Twinkle, Twinkle Little Star" or "Baa, Baa Black Sheep." First sing it in a happy voice, then a sad voice. You could also try a frustrated voice, hurt voice, shy voice, or excited voice. Let your child identify the feeling, providing cues and help if needed.

Teacher Technique for
Learning to Recognize and Name Emotions

FEELINGS PICTURES

AGES: 3–5

Materials: Index cards, markers

Preparation: Draw simple pictures on index cards of faces showing different emotions (happy, sad, startled, confused, frustrated). Or use the faces on page 128, copying and enlarging them to fit on an index card.

What to Do: Describe an event for your child and ask him to pick the face that shows what the person might be feeling.

Variation: Point at people's faces in books and magazines and ask your child to identify how he thinks the person is feeling.

Teacher Technique for **Expressing Emotions**

STREAMER STICKS

AGES: 4–6

Materials: Craft sticks, tape, crepe paper streamers, music with varying tempos

Preparation: Cut six to eight 15-inch streamers. Twist the bunch together at one end and tape the twisted ends to one side of a wooden craft stick.

What to Do: Explain to your child that you are going to dance to different types of music and make your streamer stick dance to the music, too. Play a variety of music, including pieces that are fast, slow, loud, soft, gentle, or deep. Encourage your child to make the streamer stick follow the music. While dancing, ask: "How does this music make you feel?" or "Can you name a feeling that goes with this music?"

Variations: Staple or tape colorful scarves to a wooden ruler or dowel stick.

Understanding That Feelings Change

Young children don't always have the experience to recognize that feelings change, sometimes many times over the course of a day. In the classroom or at home, children might react very emotionally to feelings of sadness or disappointment because they don't realize the feeling is temporary and they'll be able to feel happy again soon. The sad feels as if it will last forever. Guiding your child toward an understanding of the very basic concept that *feelings change* is a key step toward helping him understand and manage his emotions.

One way to do this is simply to comment on the change, adding the simple reminder: "Feelings change." "You were disappointed when we couldn't go to the park. Now you're having fun playing in the yard. Feelings change." Don't belabor the point or force your child to agree—simply make the observation and move on.

In her Maryland kindergarten classroom, Dara Feldman used pictures of children in various emotional states—happy, frustrated, sad, lonely—to create an Emotions Board. Her students would put their name above the picture to show what they were feeling at any point during the day, and were encouraged to move their name when their feelings changed.

Teacher Technique for **Understanding That Feelings Change**

FACES AND FEELINGS

AGES: 3–6

Materials: White letter-size envelope, index cards, markers, scissors, glue

Preparation: Cut one end off the envelope to form a pocket. Draw faces on the top half of the index cards—these could include happy, sad, confused, sleepy, or silly. Or copy and enlarge the feeling faces below and glue each onto an index card. Write your child's name on the envelope and decorate it.

What to Do: Hang the decorated envelope on a bulletin board or wall with the open pocket at the top so it forms a pouch. Place the "feeling faces" index cards nearby. Each morning, allow your child to select a card with the face best showing how she feels, and place it into the pouch, face side up. Encourage her to change the face as her feelings change during the day.

Variation: Place a magnetic photo frame on your refrigerator—your child can place the picture of the feeling face in the frame, and change as needed.

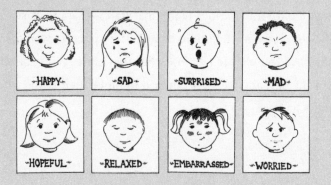

FEELINGS JAR

AGES: 5–6

Materials: A fish bowl, jar, flower vase, or decorative dish; craft sticks

Preparation: Draw faces of various feelings on the craft sticks. Place them in a basket near the bowl or dish, which you can label "Feelings Jar."

What to Do: Have your child simply drop a stick showing whatever emotion she is feeling into the jar. You can go through them together at the end of the day. The point is simply to recognize the wide range of feelings a person can have in a day. (Be certain to have several sticks with each emotion, so they're available even if she has already "used" the happy or sad or excited face.)

Understanding the Difference
Between Feelings and Actions

An action can cause a feeling. But a feeling cannot cause an action.

This is difficult territory, difficult even for some adults to successfully navigate. But it's essential for your child to understand if she's to learn the important skills of managing her emotions and solving her own problems.

The lesson good teachers emphasize is this: There is a difference between feelings and actions. A child might feel happy or sad, disappointed or excited, based on how someone acts toward him. But that *feeling* cannot make him *do* anything—he decides what to do.

You could use children's storybooks to illustrate the concept that feelings are different from actions. Teachers frequently read stories to their students and talk about what the characters felt and how they acted. After reading a story to your child, talk about it together. "How did the Little Engine That Could feel when he saw the big hill?" Then ask: "What did he do?"

To help your child separate her own feelings from her actions, first help her identify the feeling and then guide her toward some possible actions. "It looks like you're sad because you want to play with that doll. Do you want to ask Kate for a turn, or should we look around for another doll to play with?"

You can also gently guide your child after the fact, pointing out her feeling and the behavior she chose and other possible choices: "You looked pretty sad when you didn't get a chance to play with the doll. I wonder what would have happened if you asked Kate for a turn?"

Learning Self-Soothing, or Relaxation Techniques

Understanding feelings is, of course, different from actually *feeling* sad or angry or disappointed. Children naturally look to the adults around them for comfort when things go wrong. There is perhaps nothing more important for a young child's sense of emotional security than knowing someone is there for her when she's feeling alone.

However, as your child gets better at identifying and understanding his emotions, it's also valuable for him to learn some tricks to comfort himself. To help, as you comfort your child, you can also teach him some ways he can do the same for himself.

Here are some self-soothing techniques often used to prevent melt-down situations or deal with escalating frustrations in early childhood classrooms:

- When your child starts feeling frustrated or upset (but before she has melted down completely), suggest that she get a drink of water or go wash her hands. Water tends to be a natural soother for young children.

- Touch is very soothing and important for young children, if they're receptive to it. In the classroom, when a child is upset, a teacher might touch his arm or shoulder before asking: "Is there something I can do to help you?" She might touch or hold his hand, or put an arm on his back while reassuring: "We can work through this together." At home, you can give your child a back rub or massage his shoulders, or scratch his back. If this is helpful to your child, you could also teach him self-massage techniques. Have him stretch out his legs and rub them, or rub his arms. Similarly, you could teach him to "give himself a hug" by wrapping his arms around himself. However, it's important to respect your child's limits when it comes to touch. Some children don't like being touched when they're already frustrated or emotional. If your child pulls away from you, or otherwise indicates this technique is not working, respect that boundary.

- Make up a short poem or chant your child can use to calm herself during stressful times. (The Rice family uses: "I can do it! I'm okay! I can manage anyway!")

- Once a child appears to be soothed—the initial intense emotion has passed—good teachers find it is helpful to give a simple task to make sure the child is back on track and has a good sense of internal organization. You might ask your child to build a simple puzzle, sort a handful of buttons into piles, count coins, or make a simple block tower. Explain why he is doing this, and tell him it's a good idea to give himself a simple task after handling a strong emotion, just to be sure he's ready to move on.

Oregon teacher Jackie Cooke has a "safe place" set aside in her classroom for children who are feeling out of control or emotional. There she has a basket that contains squeezable stress balls and small stuffed animals. She has attached little labels to each of the stuffed animals that remind students of different stress releasers and self-calming techniques that she teaches and the students practice throughout the year, such as "Tighten and relax your muscles" or "Count backward from 100" or "Visualize a calm place." Children may occasionally be asked to go to the "safe place" if they are losing emotional control, or they may choose to go there on their own at any point.

After discussing relaxation techniques with her class, Mrs. Rice posts a chart in her classroom that reads:

When you are frustrated, you could:
- Walk to another area of the room to begin a new activity.
- Ask to take a drink or bathroom break.
- Count to 10.
- Find a teacher or other adult.
- Get your journal to write about it.
- Go to the library center and pull out a book and a pillow.
- Breathe, breathe, breathe.

COMFY CORNER

AGES: 3–6

Materials: Large blanket, small rug, or pillows

Preparation: With your child, find an area that is quiet and away from distraction such as a corner of a room, behind a couch, or under a table. Put a small rug or pillow in the area. You can also add a CD player with relaxing music.

What to Do: Explain the purpose of the area, showing her how peaceful it is. Suggest times she might want to use it. (Your child should never be forced to use this area, nor placed there as punishment.)

Teacher Technique for
Easing a Child's Frustration and Stress

RAIN STICKS

AGES: 3–6

Materials: Long, cardboard tube (one from a roll of gift wrap), dry rice (about 3/4 cup), markers, stickers, plastic wrap, tape, rubber bands

Preparation: With your child, decorate the tube as desired. Cover one end with plastic wrap and secure with tape. Put 1–2 rubber bands around the end to firmly secure the plastic wrap. Pour the rice into the open end. Seal the open end with the plastic wrap, tape, and rubber bands.

What to Do: Demonstrate for your child that when the tube is turned, the rice falls from one end to the other like rain. If the tube is tipped slowly, the rice will fall slowly and softly. If the tube is tipped quickly, the rice will fall quickly and loudly. When your child feels stressed, you can suggest that she listen to the soothing sounds of the rain stick.

BLOW A BALLOON

AGES: 3–5

Materials: None

Preparation: None.

What to Do: If your child is tense, angry, or feeling out of control, explain that it's time to blow up a balloon. Then pretend to hold a balloon to your mouth and blow. Have your child do the same. Make it bigger, bigger, and bigger. Each time, inhale and blow while pretending that the balloon grows larger. Then, *pop*, it falls to the floor. Repeat as needed.

Variation: Label a jar of lotion with a soothing scent (such as lavender) as "Calming Cream" or "Relaxing Lotion." Show your child how to rub the lotion on his arms or legs when he is feeling upset, giving himself a small massage while enjoying the calming scent.

Teaching and Using Relaxation and Visualization Techniques

It's important to teach children techniques to relax their bodies and release their anxiety before they actually need to use the techniques. Patti Teel is a former special education teacher and music specialist dubbed "The Dream Maker" for her work teaching parents how to use relaxation and visualization techniques to help their children sleep. She often visits early childhood classrooms to help young children learn relaxation and visualization techniques.

To teach these techniques at home, Ms. Teel advises parents to first teach their young children how to tense and then relax the muscles throughout their bodies. One fun way to do this is to have your child imagine she is a marionette attached to a string, then name the body part she should tense and relax, starting at her head and working down to her toes. Or you might have her imagine she is a statue, making each of her muscles as firm as stone, and then relaxing them. The child should keep the muscle tense for a few seconds before relaxing it completely.

The next step is to teach your child to concentrate on her breathing. Ms. Teel sometimes first has children put their hands on their heart and feel it beat. She then sometimes leads them through an exercise where they visualize the love they have in their hearts: for themselves, for their classmates (or the people around them), and for the world. Then she asks them to feel each breath going in and out of their bodies. She sometimes has them imagine having a small weight on their bellies, and feeling it go up and down with each breath. Or she asks them to imagine a balloon in their bellies, feeling it expand with each exhale and flatten with each inhale.

"Children have to learn how to relax their bodies first, and then they can learn how to do visualization," she explains.

Visualization techniques involve having your child imagine being in a calm place, perhaps on a quiet beach, or up on a cloud. A visualization is essentially a story that is calming and relaxing. Ms. Teel has written visualizations that involve going through a forest, drifting down a river, or growing like a seed.

Patrice McCrary uses breathing and visualization techniques in simple, everyday ways in her Kentucky classroom.

"An example might be if we are running a bit late for lunch and I have not had the time to pull the children together after a busy activity," she says. "Very quickly, I will have them close their eyes and take three deep breaths. Then I have them picture themselves sitting nicely in the lunchroom, visiting with a friend, eating. I find this really helps."

If your child responds well to relaxation and visualization techniques, you can teach him to use the techniques when he is feeling frustrated or anxious. The steps would be to (1) tense and release his muscles to calm his body, (2) then concentrate on his breathing, taking deep and calming breaths, and (3) imagine being in a calm and relaxing place that he has practiced visualizing with you.

And remember, these techniques should be taught and practiced at times when your child is calm and receptive, not when he is already stressed or losing control of his emotions.

If Frustration Gets the Better of You...

You also should have some simple techniques you use when frustration starts to get the better of you: Briefly walk outside or to a window, explaining to your child, "I need a moment for myself," or listen to relaxing music.

Ms. Teel suggests imagining yourself as a "silent witness" or a "calm observer," detached and watching without anger or judgment. Practice this technique when a situation calls for a calm response, not immediate action. Another technique is to imagine a small mirror attached to your child's forehead, just above her eyes. When you feel yourself acting frustrated or losing control, picture your reflection in that mirror, recognizing that this is what your child sees. Try to react in the way you want to be seen.

If you find you're having repeated problems keeping your patience with your child, you could find it helpful to write down ten positive things about your child each day. Teachers sometimes do this with children who test their patience. Write these down every evening for at least one week. The act of doing this—focusing on your child's strengths—helps you see him in a different light and respond to him differently, which will also positively affect his self-image and behavior.

Similarly, you could post a picture of yourself and your child during a happy and cooperative time in a prominent place in your home. Seeing the picture daily could help you both revise your self-images and responses—and it will at least make you smile.

In Kentucky, Mrs. McCrary uses the techniques she teaches her students—and more. "I laugh, breathe, and visualize. In other words, I practice what I preach," she says.

"Every day something funny happens. On the days when I get to school a little tired and I have meetings lined up every afternoon for the next week, I sometimes find that I literally have to put a smile on my face as I get out of my car in the parking lot. I have found that I can 'fake it until I make it.' By the time the children step through the door of our classroom, I have a genuine smile on my face, ready to greet each one by name and with a hug."

Learning to Find Solutions

In the classroom, good early childhood teachers integrate problem-solving skills throughout their day. The goal is to teach your child ways to find solutions to her problems, rather than expecting you to solve them. There are two keys to remember: (1) You need to help your child understand the difference between problems she might be able to solve herself and ones that require help, and (2) you need to guide her through the process, helping her verbalize the problem and possible solutions.

In teaching problem-solving skills, good classroom teachers find that one helpful technique is to start the process *away* from the context of actually resolving conflict, just helping their students brainstorm for ways to use objects or do something differently. At home, you might ask your young child to come up with five ways to use an empty shoe box (they might decide to store toys in it, poke holes in it and play with it in the sandbox, use it as a cookie jar, put old shoes in it and throw it away, or wrap a present in it). The answer doesn't matter—the idea is simply to become good at looking at different ways to approach things, and to inspire your child's creative thinking and confidence.

Here are some other ideas you can use in this exercise. Brainstorm for five ways to:

- Say good-bye.
- Pet the dog.
- Use an empty paper towel roll.
- Wipe up a spill.
- Use an empty milk jug.

Once your child becomes good at brainstorming, you can talk about possible problems he might face and ways to solve them.

In Mrs. Rice's kindergarten classroom, she spends time on problem solving before she introduces any new activity. For example, before the start of the first group "carpet time," she asks what types of situations might cause problems at the carpet. The children may say, "Someone is poking me," or "Someone is talking," or "Someone is in my way." She writes each possible problem on a large piece of paper titled "At the Carpet." Any problems that the group feels should be only handled by a grown-up are starred with a red marker. (For example, "Someone is bleeding," "Someone has gotten sick," or perhaps, "Someone is crying.")

As a group, they then go on to talk about and act out possible solutions to the other problems. Acting out the solution is a key to teaching problem-solving skills. They will practice saying aloud, as a group or individually, some words they could use to handle each problem.

For instance, if the problem is "Someone keeps talking to me," the group might first try out the solution: Look in the opposite direction and count to ten without saying anything to the person. "We discuss: If this works, our problem is solved!" Mrs. Rice explains. "Otherwise, we have to try another approach."

Next, they might try the solution of *saying:* "Stop. I'm trying to listen and I can't." They practice saying this in a calm, firm voice. Once again, they discuss that if this works and the child stops talking to them, their problem has been solved. Otherwise, they should try again.

Another solution might be: I will move away to the front, back, left, or right to get out of the way. If a teacher notices me or asks why I'm moving, I will say, "I'm being bothered and I'm moving away." The group then practices not only the movement away, but also the telling of the problem to the teacher if questioned.

If it works, the problem is solved. If none of the three possible solutions has worked, it's time to get help. Mrs. Rice gives the children this guideline for seeking help solving their problems: "Try three, then get me."

As a group, they repeat this problem-solving process throughout the first weeks of school, focusing on a different time or area of the classroom each time. They create charts showing possible solutions for:

- Problems that might occur at the group carpet
- Problems that might occur at our tables

- Problems at playtime
- Problems in line or the hallway
- Problems in the bathroom
- Problems in the lunchroom
- Problems at outdoor recess

At home, you could develop similar lists with your child of possible problems that might happen when a friend comes over to play, when she goes to the playground, or when her brother wants a toy she is playing with.

Here are some examples of problem charts you might want to make with your child.

At a friend's house:
- Your friend won't let you play with one of his toys.
- You are served a food you don't like.
- You suddenly feel homesick or want to go home.

In the grocery store:
- You are told you can't have something you really want.
- Your parent is talking to someone and you're waiting a really long time.
- You get lost.

When a friend comes over:
- Your friend wants to play with a toy that is special to you.

- Your friend wants to do something that you're not allowed to do in your house.
- Your little brother won't leave you and your friend alone.

Remember to:

1. Discuss what problems could occur. Write them down.
2. Decide if it's a problem that a child could handle alone. If so, think of a possible solution and act it out.
3. Think about whether the solution might have worked. If not, try again.

When practicing problem-solving skills at home with your child, it's important to give her specific words or phrases she can use. For example, when someone is trying to grab a toy away, you can say: "You can tell him to stop. Tell him you're not finished playing with that yet."

Mrs. Rice also writes each problem on a slip of paper to put in a class "problem-solving jar." During a free moment, she will pick a slip from the jar and the children will act out possible solutions to the problem again. You could do the same at home, going through one or two problems each evening. Be sure to include a few problems that would require a child to get an adult's help, so your child understands there are some problems she's not expected to solve on her own.

In Hawaii, Pauline Jacroux has her students role-play everything from introducing their parents at open house to resolving a playground dispute. "How should you say 'Stop it' to someone who is annoying you?" she asks. "Don't just whine 'Stooppppppp it.' You look them in the eye and say, 'Stop it, I don't like it when you do that.' We practice the day-to-day things. It's just basic little behaviors. We're going to practice: Pretend he has just hit you on the playground. We practice: What do you do if something happens by accident? To teach this, you practice and you role-play."

Once you've practiced problem-solving skills with your child, here are some other techniques you can use when your child approaches you with a problem or complaint:

- Simply ask, "How did you solve it?" and listen to her response. She may have already come up with her own solution, and just needs to tell you about it. In this case, acknowledge her accomplishment: "Great job! I knew you could do it!" If she responds with a shrug of her shoulders or no response, she's not confident about solving the problem on her own. You could offer some choices: "Think about whether you want to ignore him or tell him to stop. If you need me near when you try, let me know."

- Suggest that he write it down on a piece of paper, drawing a picture or face that shows the problem or how he is feeling. Then you can sit down together to look at the picture and discuss it. Your child could draw some possible solutions to the problem, or you might write them down together, or you could just talk about them.

Teaching the Basics of Conflict Resolution

You also could teach your child the basic steps of conflict resolution, and perhaps set up a spot where she can use this technique. Teachers who use conflict resolution in the classroom generally use this basic model: Both parties meet in a calm spot. One at a time, each describes the problem. They come up with ideas for solving the problem. Once they reach a solution they both like, they agree to give it a try.

In Mrs. Rice's classroom, she has set up a "Peace Table" on a small snack table in the corner of the room where the children can use this conflict resolution technique. The procedure of conflict resolution is posted there:

1. Describe the problem.
2. Think of ideas to solve the problem.
3. Decide on a solution you both like.
4. Go give it a try.

It's important for the children to understand that only one person can talk at a time and the other person should listen. At Mrs. Rice's Peace Table, she has a fancy pencil for the "talking" person to hold, then hand to the other person when he's through.

At home, you might use conflict resolution with bickering siblings, or playmates who are having a difficult time. Remember that when children use conflict resolution, it's important for an adult to follow up with them later to see if their solution worked.

"PICK" A SOLUTION

AGES: 4–6

Materials: Plastic or silk flowers with stems; vase or plant pot; rice, sand, or marbles; slips of paper; tape

Preparation: On small slips of paper, write various solutions to common problems. Tape one slip of paper to the upper part of each flower's stem. Fill the vase or pot with the sand, rice, or marbles. Place the flowers into the vase.

What to Do: When your child approaches you with a problem that needs to be solved, have your child "pick" a solution. If she doesn't like it, or it doesn't work, she can pick again until she finds an appropriate solution.

Variation: Make a flower center, stem, and petals out of construction paper. Write solutions on the petals, and tape them to the flower stem. Glue onto paper or poster board. Hang in a common area. When your child approaches you with a problem, have your child "pick" a petal suggesting a solution. She can either try it, or pick again.

Managing Emotions and Conflict Through Stories

Another way to help empower your child to figure out solutions to problems is by telling stories. Young children love stories, and they especially love stories made up by the people they love. Mrs. Cooke, whom we met earlier in this chapter, began writing stories for her young grandchildren and she now uses those stories in lessons for her kindergartners.

Mrs. Cooke's stories often feature herself and her sister *as children* as the main characters. Usually, they're overcoming some obstacle or learning an important character trait. Often, her stories are framed as a "story within a story," for instance, about a young boy struggling after starting school in a new classroom, and how a teacher tells him a story about the time she and her sister learned the meaning of "perseverance."

When making up stories for your children, Mrs. Cooke suggests that you be willing to tell the naughty stuff you did as a child. "It helps children relate and feel better when they know someone they admire can admit to not being perfect—and was once a child just like them!" she says.

Mrs. Cooke also suggests including your child's thoughts or suggestions in the story wherever possible. With her grandchildren, they created the stories together. In the classroom, if a child interrupts with a comment or question, she weaves that into the story.

And she recommends talking about the story afterward. Her stories include discussion questions she uses for her students to share their own experiences. Afterward, they go back to their desks and write some of their personal stories in their journals.

Here are some other guidelines for making up your own stories:

- Although children enjoy "recognizing" characters in stories, it's best not to use your own child as the story's main character, as this can feel intimidating and controlling.
- Keep the "solutions" positive and helpful—for example, you shouldn't make up a story about a boy who won't listen to his mom and then encounters serious harm.

If you're not comfortable making up your own stories, another fun and easy technique is to make up the stories together as a game. You and your child could begin playing the "Story Game" together once your child is about four. Your child would begin by creating a character. You would add a sentence creating a problem the character is facing. Your child would describe the character's feelings as they face their problem. You would create a solution. And your child would end with a feeling.

The story might look something like this:

Child: There was a dolphin named Danny who lived in the ocean.
Adult: Danny did not know how to swim.
Child: This made Danny very sad.
Adult: So one day, Danny went to the YMCA and took swim classes.
Child: Danny was very proud.

Remember, the format looks like this: *Child: Character. Adult: Problem. Child: Feeling. Adult: Solution. Child: Feeling.* Once you've played a few times, you could switch roles.

Is It Tattling or Problem Solving?

On a final note, every day in the classroom, teachers are confronted with problems like these:

> "Madison didn't clean up the blocks after she was done playing."
>
> "Jake called Alex a poopy-head!"
>
> "Freddy wasn't listening during story time. He was playing with his watch instead!"

The basic format is: Somebody else did something. Some people call this tattle-telling, as in "Don't be a tattletale!" or "That's tattling." But good early childhood teachers recognize this as another step along the path toward problem solving, and one that should be respected rather than diminished or discouraged.

When your child comes to you with complaints about someone else's behavior, it is her way of expressing that something is not "fair," or that she recognizes someone is not behaving as he should. This is one of the ways children move away from egocentrism—thinking of themselves as the center of the world—and toward making sense of other people's actions and points of view.

As your child's guide, you should help him to recognize when something is a problem he can solve, when he should bring it to an adult's attention, and when he can safely ignore the behavior and move on. But recognize that these are not easy lessons, and your child should be allowed to turn to an adult with more experience to help him.

Think of it from another perspective: As an adult, you are sometimes confronted with problems that are beyond your authority to resolve—if you saw a drunken driver speeding down the road, it would be safer and more effective to call the police than to chase them down and take away their car keys. Or imagine if you came home from work and were telling your spouse about a rough day you had with a coworker. You're not expecting your spouse to go talk to your boss or find you a new job or call a therapist for you. And you surely wouldn't expect your spouse to respond: "That's tattling."

Sometimes children come to you with problems because they don't have the ability or authority to solve them on their own. Other times they tell you their complaints because they simply need someone to talk to. Be respectful of these needs.

If you feel your child is approaching you with a problem she could have handled on her own, you could respond: "That sounds tough. What did you do to handle it?" If she's complaining about something, you could tell her: "What a difficult time you had! I'm glad to see you're still so calm!"

We spend lots of time teaching our children to feed themselves, dress themselves, go to the bathroom themselves, and read by themselves. We expect that our children will master these skills with our teaching, practicing, and modeling. Why should solving problems be different?

As Mrs. Seay notes: "If your child couldn't tie her shoes, you wouldn't punish her for that. You would keep teaching her, practicing, modeling for her." Problem-solving skills, like the others, must be taught, practiced, and reinforced.

8

THE IMPORTANCE
OF PLAY

Why and How You Should Play with
Your Young Child Every Day

Everyone knows that children play. But why? Is it simply a fun way to pass the time? A distraction? Or something more?

The nation's best early childhood teachers understand there's a deep, vital relationship between young children and play—that play is absolutely essential for young children. In fact, it would be almost impossible for a healthy child *not* to play.

This relationship is often described by saying: Play is like a child's work, or more famously, Play is the work of childhood. While this explanation certainly emphasizes that play is important, it also somehow muddies things up, making it difficult to grasp the role of play in a child's life. Yes, adults generally do have to work, and in that regard their work could be considered essential. And yet, adult work can be routine, predictable, or unfulfilling—the exact opposite of what play is to a child.

I glimpsed the relationship between children and play while I was writing this book and my youngest daughter Lucille was diagnosed with a congenital heart defect. She had to undergo heart surgery at age two. When she awoke from the surgery, connected to tubes and monitors in her hospital bed, her first question was: "Can I get down and play?"

Of course, she could not. But as her body began to heal, she was able to get down, first to sit awkwardly in my arms as I read her stories, and then, finally, to visit one of the hospital's many playrooms. There, attached to a portable heart monitor and moving gingerly, she picked up a tiny plastic "girl" and walked her through a dollhouse. That visit was a turning point for Lucille. Once back to the essential business of play, she began to heal even more quickly, heading off to the playroom several times a day.

She was being treated at an excellent children's hospital that clearly recognized the significance of play in children's lives. There was a very important rule for the hospital playrooms, a principle really: No doctors or nurses or technicians were allowed to come into a playroom and do any medical procedure on a child. They could not take blood, they could not administer medicine, they could not even take a child's temperature. The playroom was a place where children felt safe. Play was not merely a way to distract a child from the "real" business of medicine, but something valuable and healing all on its own.

Watching Lucille play, watching her toddle off to feed her baby doll dressed in an identical hospital gown, I realized that a child's play is like an adult's work if that adult is, perhaps, an artist and his work is painting, or if that adult is a composer and his work is making music. Play is how children make sense of their world. It is a deep, instinctive, and creative drive. An artist, perhaps, would rush from his hospital bed to his easel and his healing would be speeded there. But most adult work could not touch this. Play is how children see and understand the world—how they control things they cannot yet affect, how they learn about themselves and their passions, how they grow and adapt and become capable and strong.

A few days after Lucille was released from the hospital, I took my four-year-old son Jack along to pick my older daughter Maya, then seven, up from school. It was a beautiful fall afternoon. Maya, with Jack and her best friend, Kate, ran through an open field near the school. They started playing a game that looked like this: One would lie down on the ground. The other two would lean over the first. Then the child lying on the ground would get up, arms stuck out straight, and chase the other two around the field. The person who was caught would then lie on the ground and the sequence would repeat itself.

When I called the kids back to me to head home, Maya said, "We were playing the most fun game ever!" And she explained the game was called Heart Surgery. The person lying on the ground was the patient. The other two were doctors who leaned over the patient and removed the patient's heart from his body. And the patient would get up in a zombie-like fashion and chase the doctors.

I hesitated. She was happy, clearly having fun. And yet it was important to me that she and her brother understood Lucille's surgery as much as possible. I had worried so much about how it might affect them, what they might think, what might scare or disturb them. I opened my mouth to say something, and paused. Maya immediately interrupted.

"We know that's not how heart surgery really works," she said happily. "It was just so much fun to play." And I knew everything was going to be okay. They were coming to terms with the surgery in their own way, through play.

What Is "True Play" and Why Is It Important?

Every day in the classroom, good teachers see the importance of play. They teach through play. They learn about their students through play. And they help children understand themselves and each other through play.

Play is simple, really. And yet, because it's so important on so many different levels, it's become confusing and at times even overwhelming to us as parents. Since young children learn through play, it's become natural to assume we should be using their playtime to teach them—colors, letters, shapes, words, and more. We have computer programs to help, and almost every toy in the stores has a "smart" computer chip that teaches something important. And if that's not enough, there are music classes, organized sports, even play classes where you can schedule play (and learning!) right into your child's week.

But that's not what good early childhood teachers mean when they talk about play. Although teachers do integrate play into almost all of their classroom lessons—in other words, they make their lessons play-based—when they talk about the value of play, they're referring to something they call "true play" (or "free play" or "child-directed play"). These terms are a teacher's way of saying that your child should be using her imagination while she plays, and she should be actively engaged in creating the play rather than passively responding to prompts or operating within predetermined limits.

Play is not the same thing as having fun. A music or gymnastics class can be fun and beneficial for your child. But it is not the same as true play. Similarly, organized sports would not meet the definition of true play. Nor would computer games—though all of these things can certainly benefit a child.

A child engaged in true play might use wooden blocks to build a structure that becomes a zoo for toy animals or a roadway for race cars. He might be cutting play dough into pretend pies that he then sells at a pretend bake sale. There's an element of imagination involved, and the play could take him in a direction he didn't originally imagine. There's no real beginning or end to his play, because it is so adaptable.

This concept of "true play" is so important that the American Academy of Pediatrics issued a policy statement in 2006 emphasizing the need to preserve this type of play as an essential part of childhood. The AAP report notes that "Play is so important to optimal child

If You Have More Than One Child

It's important to spend time playing with each child individually, as well as playing together as a family. Recognize that your children may have different interests and abilities, but do try to find some games or play activities you all can enjoy together.

development that it has been recognized by the United Nations High Commission for Human Rights as a right of every child."

The report recommends "blocks and dolls, with which children use their imagination fully, over passive toys that require limited imagination," and notes that "parents who share unscheduled spontaneous time with their children are being wonderfully supportive, nurturing and productive."

Why Should You Play with Your Child?

While true play is "child-directed," it's important to note that this does not mean "without adult involvement." The best teachers do not see the children's playtime as a time to leave the kids alone while they grade papers or catch up on paperwork. As much as possible, they try to play *with* the students at least daily, taking advantage of the chance to have meaningful one-on-one interactions with them.

The nature of your child's play can give you a great window into how she thinks and functions in the world. Playing with your child can teach you more about her—and give you more opportunities to impact her behavior and growth—than almost any other interaction you could have. (This understanding may date all the way back to Plato, who said: "You can discover more about a person in an hour of play than in a year of conversation.")

When playing with your child, you could try to note how much detail she gives to her play—is the play rich and imaginative, or is it difficult for her to create play scenarios or fully engage herself in her play? The level of detail a child gives to play tells you a lot about her attention span and ability to adapt to different learning situations.

Interestingly, the relationship works both ways: A child who provides a great deal of detail to her play tends to have a greater attention span, and better language and literacy skills—and by guiding your child to add more detail to her play, you can help increase these abilities.

The NAEYC notes in its position statement on developmentally appropriate practice in early childhood classrooms: "Research demonstrates the importance of sociodramatic play as a tool for learning curriculum content with 3- through 6-year-old children. When teachers provide a thematic organization for play; offer appropriate play props, space and time; and become involved in the play by extending and elaborating on children's ideas, children's language and literacy skills can be enhanced."

This is why good early childhood classrooms are filled with lots of play props, and why the teachers provide suggestions to move play to a "higher level," which is more varied, complex, and detailed. You can do the same at home, with tips we'll outline below. In addition, by playing with your child, you can:

- Help guide her through difficult or stressful situations.
- Teach her the basics of getting along with others—how to make friends and how to be a friend.
- Show her that she can trust you, that you are someone who cares about her, someone who pays attention to her, and someone she can rely upon.

The Levels of Play

To understand your child's play, it may first be helpful to know that there are levels and stages of play. As far back as 1933, psychologist Mildred Parten identified six levels of play, which she said preschool-age children move through sequentially (her categories were: unoccupied behavior, onlooker, solitary play, parallel play, associative play, cooperative play). These levels have been studied, modified, and redefined through the decades, but the basic concept has remained the same: Children's play moves along a spectrum from playing alone to being able to play with other children and groups of children. To help understand play levels, here is one simple version that guides early childhood teachers in the classroom:

1. Playing alone, reached in infancy, when a baby first finds her toes and plays with them or bats at a mobile above her crib or coos to herself.

2. Playing with an adult, reached in infancy, when a parent gently tickles her baby and she giggles, or they play Pat-a-Cake.

3. Playing *next to* another child, also known as "parallel play," reached around age thirteen to fifteen months. The children enjoy each other's presence, but they are each playing on their own. For instance, they may both be playing with blocks, but each is building his own tower.

4. Playing *with* another child, usually reached around age two, when children play the same activity together, interacting with each other and directly affecting each other's play. Now they might build something together with the blocks.

5. Playing within a small group of three or four children, usually reached around age three. As in parallel play, the children each share a link in the "story" of whatever they're playing.

6. Playing within a large group of five or more kids, usually reached around age five—perhaps building with blocks and then pretending it is a zoo, or creating a post office and writing and delivering letters.

Once a child has mastered one level of play, he can easily move among the previous levels as well. For example, a child who is able to play within a small group of children can also easily play by herself or with an adult. Children frequently shift among levels of play throughout the day. The difficulty comes in moving on to the next level. So the child who is comfortable playing with one close friend may still have difficulties trying to play within a small group.

Why is it helpful to know this? Because some problems commonly defined as misbehavior or disobedience are really the result of a child being expected to play or interact at a level she hasn't yet mastered. These children become frustrated and overwhelmed, and may act in ways that would lead you to believe they "can't share" or "don't know how to play."

In the classroom, early childhood teachers use observation skills to determine what level of play a child has reached. Entire teacher textbooks have been written on observing children's play, but the concept really is simple: Watch. If your three-year-old quickly becomes overwhelmed or frustrated playing in a small group of other kids, be nearby to offer guidance or support. Respect his abilities and limitations. Take small steps, and model appropriate play behaviors (sharing, taking turns, listening). This does not need to be complicated or overwhelming—simply know that children move through different levels of play, and that making the jump from one level to the next can be difficult.

Influencing the Detail of Your Child's Play

When you play with your child, you should understand that while you want to keep the play child-centered, young children often do need someone to model ways to play for them. Even a child who loves Dora the Explorer might not know that she can take her new Dora doll along with her on adventures, hiding under the table, going outside and filling her backpack with rocks, "camping out" in a tent made of a towel. You can guide her to these types of activities, rather than watching her simply tote her new doll from room to room, or leave it lying on her bed.

By engaging in your child's play and modeling ways to play, you can guide her to the "higher level" of play discussed earlier, which involves more detail, more creativity, and more variety. Remember your goal is not to take over your child's play—you do not want to direct it or change it. You're simply providing props and suggestions that will make her play deeper and more engaging.

Here are some classroom-based themes you can use to guide your child to a "higher level" of play at home, providing props and guidance while keeping play child-centered.

- If your child is playing with her stuffed animals, you might help set up a veterinarian's office, providing strips of rags to use as slings or bandages, a clipboard for taking medical notes, a notepad for prescriptions, and props from a pretend doctor's kit. You can offer to be an assistant who gets supplies for the doctor, or pretend to be an owner waiting with her pet, or pretend to take phone calls and make appointments.
- If your child is playing with blocks, you can increase the creative possibilities by providing race cars, action figures, maps, or pretend animals, so you and your child might create a roadway, a city, or a zoo. You also could add a clipboard with paper for drawing "blueprints," as well as measuring tools such as rulers or tape

measures. Block centers in early childhood classrooms also often include cardboard tubes, small boxes, scraps of fabric, hardhats, and tools.

- If your child is outside digging or finding rocks, you could help set up a "science center," where she can store and examine her favorite finds. It might include a magnifying glass, binoculars, scales, a clipboard or journal, measuring tools, paper cups and plates, magnets, and an eye dropper.

- If your child is playing with cars or trucks, you could use masking tape to create a roadway on the floor or chalk on the ground. Create a city using boxes as buildings. Empty tubes could be used to make stoplights or streets signs, or they could become logs for bulldozers to push.

- If your child is feeding her baby doll, you could suggest bringing the baby to a pretend restaurant, taking turns being the waiter and bringing food to the baby and parent, or you could set up some boxes in rows and bring the baby "grocery shopping."

- If your child is flipping through books, you could bring out some index cards and a stamp pad and suggest playing Library, setting the books up in rows, checking them out, returning them, and reshelving them.

- If your child is doodling, you could bring out some envelopes, shoe boxes, and a sack or doll carriage, and play Post Office. Label the shoe boxes with the names of family members or friends, and use the sack for carrying mail or the doll carriage as a delivery cart. Or you could set up a table with letterhead, envelopes, pencils, an old briefcase, some junk mail, stickers, rulers, a hole punch, tape, and other office supplies and play Office.

- If your child is coloring, you could fill her craft box with items such as cotton balls, yarn, fabric scraps, pipe cleaners, aluminum foil, ribbon, Band-Aids, masking tape, and glue. When your child has made several creations, display them on a table or hang them on a wall. Invite friends and family over for an "art show," or just enjoy the show together. Serve cookies and juice.

Notice that the common element here is providing props and suggestions geared toward your child's play interests, while allowing your child plenty of opportunity to add her own imaginative touches, to be fully engaged in the play, and to move the play in her own direction. And of course, the goal is to keep play creative and fun.

Using Play to Guide Your Child Through Stress or Difficulties

If your child is going through a difficult time or period of adjustment, anything from his parents' divorce, to a move, to starting school, you could use play to help him work through the difficulties and perhaps find solutions. Notice that these techniques would not be used during your child's "free play"—in other words, you would not barge in while your child is already playing something else, but would instead find a moment to initiate this type of play on your own.

Your goal is simply to get your child to open up and share his anxieties in a way he might not otherwise, and then sometimes gently offer possible solutions for him to consider. Some children respond really well to puppets, and would whisper a secret while playing with a gentle mouse puppet that they would never say aloud to a parent at the dinner table.

In her Ohio classroom, Mimi Brodsky Chenfeld used a floppy-eared puppy puppet named Snowball who never spoke aloud but instead whispered into her ear so she could tell her students what he said.

Over the years, she notes, he brought lonely children out of their shells, cheered children in need of kind words, and noticed children who were ignored by their classmates.

Her favorite moment came the year she had a three-year-old deaf boy named Jim in her class. The child had never spoken a word, despite intervention from speech therapists. Jim watched intently every day as Snowball sent the children off with good-bye kisses. Snowball's favorite game that year was the peek-a-boo trick, which he always flubbed—revealing his furry little face too soon each time, to the children's delight.

Jim finally said his first words that year. "Where's Snowball?"

Snowball, she says, reminds adults that children need friends who are good listeners, never leave anyone out, make them laugh, and love them no matter what.

You can create a similar puppet friend at home, being sure to give him a distinct personality and plenty of love. (See the puppet directions in Chapter 2.) Use Mrs. Brodsky Chenfeld's tricks—play games where the puppet always makes the same fun mistake, allow the puppet to whisper to you then share its words with your child, have the puppet offer your child lots of kisses and love.

Other times, you could role-play with toys. One technique teachers use when guiding children through difficulties is to have the child assume the role of the authority figure in the play, while she plays the child. For instance, if your child is worried about starting school and you have a pretend schoolhouse, you could suggest playing a game, with your child playing the teacher and you playing the new student. That way, you can play out solutions to her problems that she can then consider and respond to on her own.

Teaching Your Child How to Be a Friend and Make a Friend

As we discussed in Chapter 1, one of the most important things for your young child's growing sense of self is developing friendships. But while this desire may be natural, the ability to make and keep friends doesn't come naturally to everyone.

Your child may need guidance with simple social skills—she may not know to smile and say hello, to learn another child's name, to ask about the other child. Some children need to practice making eye contact or smiling—they may need to be told that these are social cues that tell other kids that you want to play. You might practice waving and saying, "Hi!" It also might be helpful to teach her a few ways to start talking with a child she'd like to know better. For instance, you could coach her on how to compliment another child or express interest in their play. "Hi. I like your doll. I have one at home, too."

She also should understand that other children don't always respond, simply because they don't know the best way to make friends either. Reassure her that this all gets easier with practice.

If she's receptive and ready to make the jump to small-group play, you could provide her with some "social cues" to help her join in such play. For instance, you could teach her to ask other children who are playing with something she'd like to play: "Can I have a turn when you're done?" Or she could ask: "What are you playing?" and follow up with: "I like to play with blocks, too. Can I add this one next to your tower?" Provide her with specific examples of words she can use, and practice.

In Kentucky, teacher Patrice McCrary begins teaching social skills during "circle time," when her students sit in an oval and she encourages them to look at the person who is speaking rather than always looking at her.

"That makes such a difference!" she notes. "I teach them how to make eye contact with the person speaking. I want them looking at each other—not just at the teacher."

And in South Carolina, teacher Stephanie Seay has her students practice taking turns. "We use role-playing—'That's a really cool truck. Can I take turns with you?' Then we practice taking turns using a sand timer or analog clock."

Playing with Your Child Builds
Trust and a Healthy Relationship

Most importantly, remember as you play with your child that the goal is to *play*. So often as parents, we try to turn every interaction into a "learning opportunity" or a "teaching moment." But would you want to play with someone who always said things like: "What color is the dolly's dress?" or "Is this block a square or a rectangle?"

Resist those urges. As often as possible, simply join in the play. If your daughter is playing with her stuffed dogs, rather than picking one of them up and quizzing her ("What sound does the doggie make?"), you might ask: "What game does this dog like to play?" or "What does this dog have planned for today?" These are much more appropriate questions for playtime, when your goal is to *play* with your child.

Remember that playtime is a time for you to join your child's world, and perhaps to learn more about how she thinks, interacts, and sees the world. You can use these observations to help her learn new skills or adjust to difficult situations. She may be more likely to share her thoughts and concerns through play. But if you do nothing more than feed her dolls pretend crackers for ten minutes, you've still shown your child that she is important to you, that you understand her, and that you're there for here.

If you are a person who has difficulty playing with young children, one technique some teachers use which you may find helpful is to simply describe the child's play out loud. To do this, simply be a sort of reporter describing your child's activities: "Jack is moving the tow truck down the road. He's stopping. It looks like he's going to attach the tow hook to the car." Continue if your child seems to be enjoying the interaction, but be willing to stop if he seems annoyed or distracted. Do join more fully in the play if he invites you or you feel comfortable.

9

BUILDING FAMILY
AND COMMUNITY

How Teachers Transform Their Classrooms

Thinking back on my second visit to Mrs. Rice's kindergarten classroom six weeks into the school year, I was most struck by how the kids had been transformed over a few weeks from a group of individuals who cared mostly about themselves into an actual classroom community—willing to share, work together, and care for each other. This is what we all want for our families.

The process of building these bonds involves many of the techniques we've discussed throughout this book—having jobs or tasks that contribute to the family or community, living by common rules, creating rituals and routines, understanding the basics of how to get along, playing and sharing experiences, and so on.

Building this sense of togetherness also involves recognizing that people within a community or family are different, and those differences should be accepted and cherished. In her classroom, Linda DeMino Duffy devotes lessons at the start of the school year specifically toward similarities and differences. Her talk goes something like this:

Who can show me where your brain is? How did you get your brain? Were your mom and dad able to go to a special store and order the brain they would want you to have? No, the brain you are born with is the brain you live with your entire life. It is an amazing part of your body because it helps your body work and it helps you think and feel.

But our brains are very complicated and they do not all work the same way and so we are not all the same. As we grow, we help our brain develop and that's how we learn more and more. Some of us will learn certain things quickly and some of us will have to work harder. We all learn differently and we are all good at different things. Some of you this year will become very good readers, some of you will love to work with numbers and math, some will be good artists, musicians, singers, or wonderful friends who care about the people around you.

We all have special gifts. The wonderful thing about having a special gift is that you can share it. You can help your friends learn how to do things they have trouble with. You can be the teacher. It is a very nice thing to be able to help each other.

Let's pretend that we were all the same. Would you like it if we were all purple with red hair and we all wore nothing but blue clothes? Would you like it if we all lived in the same kind of house and all drove the exact same car? I think it is great that we can all be individuals and share our special gifts with each other.

How do you think we can help each other? Do you think we all need the same thing? Would you like it if everyone had to play football at recess every day or if our library only had the same book each week for everybody to read? Sometimes we all have to do the same thing, but it is nice to have choices sometimes so we can all be individuals.

My job is to try to help you learn. But you all are not the same so some of you may need some special help that others don't need. Why is that true? (Because we are not all the same.) And sometimes you can help by sharing your special gifts with your classmates.

Similar talks at home can actually help build a sense of togetherness, whether you're discussing specific differences among family members, or just differences among people in general.

As Mrs. Duffy notes: "These types of discussions help lay the foundation for your students or your own children to understand that we are all individuals and our needs are all different. If everyone is not treated the same, it is not because we like some kids more than others but because we all have different needs."

How Family Meals Can Build Community

Teachers also practice conversational skills that contribute to a sense of community, where everyone has something important to share. In Mimi Brodsky Chenfeld's classroom, she found two questions can transform a classroom: *What else?* and *What if?*

"What else can you share about your pet gerbil? What else can we think of for our spring program? 'What else?' is not smug," she says in her essay, "In Four Easy Nudges: Everything You Need to Know About Being a Creative Teacher." "It helps us to expand our horizons and reminds us that we can never completely finish a subject or an idea."

At home, meals are a wonderful time to build a greater sense of family unity and understanding in your household, using these conversational skills. To make meals more fun and engaging, you could:

- Tell stories about when you were a child the same age your child is now. At snack time and other free moments during the day, early childhood teachers share stories about when they were children. At home, you can talk about your kindergarten teacher, or whether you went to preschool. Describe your childhood backyard or your bedroom. Talk about your least favorite food, or the rule that was the most difficult to follow in your household.
- Ask questions about your child's day. Follow up by asking what your child likes best about school or day care, and what he likes

least. You could contribute some details about your day at work, and allow your child to ask you questions, if he's interested.

- Master the teacher's art of asking open-ended questions, which will teach your child thinking skills and conversational skills—and teach you more about who your child is. One classroom trick: Rather than always "teaching" your child what you know about a topic, instead ask: "What do you know about...?"

- Pose a question of the day, formatted as "What would you do if..." In Mrs. Jacroux's classroom in Hawaii, her first-graders end each day by discussing "Three New Things I Learned Today." She suggests adapting this for home, having each family member address that topic at the dinner table every night—parents included. You'll be surprised at how much you learn! And Mrs. Jacroux would add an extra twist: Jot the comments down in a simple notebook, which will become a treasured journal where you can look back together as a family and see how you've changed and grown—and what you've learned.

You also might occasionally set the table with a fancy cloth or paper tablecloth and flowers. The meal can be a regular family meal, but changing the atmosphere will make it seem different. This would provide a great opportunity to briefly discuss good table manners and other polite behavior.

Or plan a tea party instead of having snack time. Use a real tea set, set a table with a real tablecloth, set food out on nice dishes, and invite your children to sit down with each other for "tea" (milk or juice).

Have them take turns serving themselves or each other, and then carry on a quiet conversation with each other. You also could use the tea party to celebrate each other's successes, such as learning a new skill or having a good day at school.

Around the House

In many ways, your home symbolizes your family, so it's nice to create a sense of ownership or team spirit around the house much as early childhood teachers do around the classroom. Young children love the idea of being a part of a team and seeing it reflected where they live. You can delegate fun jobs and create items that reflect your team spirit at home.

For example, kindergarten teacher Patrice McCrary in Kentucky has a classroom job that rotates among students called "classroom ambassador." As she explains: "If someone walks into our classroom, our current ambassador steps up to them, introduces themselves, and shares some information about our classroom. That child then stays near the visitor until I have the opportunity to join them.

"This is a wonderful way for the children to gain even more ownership of our classroom happenings." This is also a great job for a young child at home—or siblings could share the task, with one greeting visitors, one taking their coats or offering them a drink or snack, and one introducing everyone in the family.

ME MICROPHONE

AGES: 4–6

Materials: Empty cardboard paper towel roll, aluminum foil, black construction paper or tissue paper, glue or tape

Preparation: With your child, cover the empty cardboard roll with aluminum foil. Crumple the tissue or construction paper into a ball, and glue or tape it onto one end of the paper towel roll so it looks like a microphone. (You may need to cover it with an extra layer of black paper so it looks smooth.)

What to Do: At mealtime, hand the "Me Microphone" to one person to tell about the best part of his day. Then hand it to the next person to tell about her favorite part of the day, until each person has had a turn. Only the person holding the microphone should be talking. You could also take turns telling about the most difficult or funniest parts of your day or something you are looking forward to the next day.

In Hawaii, Pauline Jacroux's students work hard together all year creating a garden outside their classroom door: the process of weeding, planting seeds, taking care of the plants, and finally harvesting and eating the vegetables helps them grow together in ways regular classroom lessons could not.

As great as the experience of gardening as a family is, the truth is that it's also a big time commitment—and not something every family has the time to do together. So Mrs. Jacroux adapted her idea for busy families: Start simply, with "garbage gardening." As Mrs. Jacroux explains, this means: Cut the tops off carrots, put them on a plate, and watch them sprout. Or drop seeds from an eaten apple into a cup of dirt. If you have any yard at all, collect leftover fruits and vegetables, put them in the netting that onions come in, and bury them, digging them up a few weeks later to see what happened.

"This doesn't have to be hard, or take any time at all," she says. "And you can still share the fun, the excitement, of seeing something grow."

Anytime

Teachers also promote class spirit by doing group projects that link the children together as one—creating classroom banners with everyone's picture or handprint, making welcome posters for open house days, giving the class a nickname to use when calling them in from the playground, creating class T-shirts to wear on field trips. Here are ways to do the same at home.

FAMILY BANNER

AGES: 3–6

Materials: Fabric, felt, or poster board; family photos; ribbon; buttons; sequins; stickers; sticky letters; fabric paint; fabric markers; fabric glue; scissors; markers

Preparation: Cut the fabric, felt, or poster board into a desired banner shape.

What to Do: With your family, decorate the banner with your names and perhaps a photo, handprint, drawing, or signature. The date or year can be added as well.

Variations:

- Create a family welcome mat for outside your front door. Start with a solid-color carpet remnant, and use fabric paint to add your family name or the word "Welcome" and each family member's footprints.
- Make coordinating T-shirts to wear on a family outing, or decorate solid-colored baseball caps.
- Sew together old T-shirts or purchase a kit to create a family quilt.
- Come up with a fun "team" nickname you can use to refer to your family, such as the "Smith Superstars," "Rockin' Rices," "Adam's Apples," "Beach Bums," or "Zoo Crew."

FAMILY BOOK CLUB

AGES: 4–6

Materials: A book that will be read as a family, paper or notebook, pen or pencil

Preparation: Read a book aloud as a family.

What to Do: After reading a book, discuss it at a weekly meeting. You could learn about the book's author, or learn more about the time or place where the book is set. Use children's books similar to those you'd read together at regular story time, though perhaps a bit longer or more complex. Choose the book together, and keep a chart showing what books you have read as a book club. Invite grandparents to join, if you wish.

Variation: You also could create your own "easy reader" books. In Dara Feldman's Maryland kindergarten classroom, she used her digital camera to take pictures of her students being helpful, and then created books to introduce new words and reinforce the value of helpfulness. At home, you might take a picture of your child wiping down a table, sweeping the floor, and dusting. You'd use one picture per page, with simple text such as: "This is Timmy with a sponge. This is Timmy with the broom. This is Timmy with the duster." Print the pages, punch holes, and either use clasps or a three-ring binder to hold them together. Read your homemade books together.

SAY IT WITH SIGN

AGES: 4–6

Materials: None

Preparation: Learn sign language for sentences such as "I love you," "Thank you," and "You're welcome." Learn sign language for the words "father," "mother," "sister," and "brother." Learn finger spelling to spell out each other's names in sign.

What to Do: Use these words and finger spellings as a special form of communication among family members.

Variation: Learn words or phrases in a foreign language, perhaps the language of your ancestors, and use them for special greetings.

10

WHERE TO GO FROM HERE: AS YOUR CHILD GROWS AND CHANGES

Adapting the Techniques You've Mastered

As you master the teacher techniques outlined in this book, you're going to notice one very important thing: Your child is growing and changing! Some of the things that used to work may no longer hold the same magic. Some of the areas where you never used to have problems may suddenly become more difficult. And some once-unresolvable issues may somehow resolve themselves. All this is normal.

The skills you've learned—and taught your child—will remain useful and adaptable for a lifetime. However, it is important to see and understand the ways your child is changing, to adapt your techniques and continue to support your child as she grows. As your child emerges from these early childhood years of (roughly) ages three to six, she's entering an exciting new stage that will last roughly until age nine. During this period, she'll likely become more independent, more responsible, and more interested in the outside world of friends and school. (This shift will continue as she grows toward adolescence.)

Listening and Transitions

Expect your child to become more skilled at following directions. You'll still want to break your directions down into clear and manageable steps, but you can expect your child to manage quite a bit more in each step.

By the age of seven, your child also should be able to (mostly) manage the stress of routine transitions largely on his own. He can switch gears more easily, and now understands that if he's interrupted while playing or working on a project, he'll be able to come back to it later. However, as his attention span has grown, he's also become more capable of becoming engrossed in a task. This can make it harder to interrupt a creative project. Continue to provide cues before an activity needs to end, so your child has time to prepare. Give him longer blocks of time to immerse himself in activities that interest him. And do allow him to keep his project in a "safe place" to come back to later.

Scheduling and Organization

By age seven, your child could be taking over more responsibility for her own personal care and belongings. She could be responsible for putting away and organizing belongings, and she likely is developing her own systems for doing this. Your child may have a distinct preference for how her clothes are put away so she can decide what to wear, or how her collections are stored so she can play with them and put them away easily. If this is the case, allow her this responsibility, providing guidance where needed.

Your child will still need to rely upon routines and checklists, and need the structure of a schedule, but she should be taking on more responsibility for creating these herself, in a way that works for her.

Creating and Following Rules

Between the ages of about six and nine, children are very interested in rules and roles. That makes this an excellent time to involve your child in sports or other group activities that interest him. Rules are becoming very important to your child's play, and he is becoming much more skilled at handling large-group situations.

At home, this is an ideal time to revisit your household rules, allowing your child more input into the rules that guide behavior. If your rules have been quite specific, this is a good time to shift toward more general guidelines, as your child will have an easier time using and adapting these than he did before. It will also help him develop an "internal voice" to guide him.

Resolving Conflict and Handling Emotions

Your child will need continued guidance in managing her emotions and resolving conflict. However, she probably is experiencing less frustration with the tasks of everyday life, and should not be having routine tantrums or physical outbursts. The techniques in this book for helping your child understand and manage her emotions will continue to work at this age. Continue to provide guidance and support as described—naming emotions, describing actions, finding techniques that work for self-soothing and problem solving.

During these years, your child will steadily shift away from seeing herself as the center of the world toward making sense of the feelings and actions of others. As a result, around the age of seven she may start to develop a strong sense of fairness, paying close attention to how others are treated and making comparisons. Respect her need for fairness, but don't allow it to dictate your own understanding of what is fair. Allow your child to express when she feels someone is being treated unfairly, and discuss some ways that fair and equal are not always the same.

Playing and Building Community

Play continues to be important in the lives of seven- to nine-year-olds. Your child will need large chunks of unscheduled and undirected time. Because of the focus on rules at this age, he will become more interested in playing games—both board games and outdoor sports games. You may notice your child and his friends creating elaborate rules-based games that only they can understand.

Your child likely will become more engrossed in an activity that appeals to him—crafts, sports, cooking, or other creative endeavors. Provide opportunities for him to explore his passions, but be careful not to overschedule him with too many organized sports or lessons. Unstructured playtime to discover and grow is still extremely important.

Your child's growing sense of fairness and his growing awareness of the world outside his home make this an excellent time to involve your family more in the outside community—volunteering at the local Humane Society, collecting can pull-tabs for the Ronald McDonald House, or donating toys and food to poor families. This will also help contribute to a strong sense of family and community.

Off You Go

As you find the tools that work for you and your child, remember to have confidence in your parenting and decisions. Dara Feldman, the Maryland kindergarten teacher, offers this thought on how she measured her teaching success. You may want to apply it at home:

"I had two essential questions every day when I walked out the door. Are my kids happy, and did they learn something worthwhile?" she says. "But most of all, I wanted them to know that they were loved—that they were loved, and that they could trust me."

TEACHER BIOGRAPHIES

Mimi Brodsky Chenfeld has been an early childhood teacher for more than fifty years, and continues to teach young children in central Ohio. Her books, including *Celebrating Young Children and Their Teachers* and *Teaching by Heart: For Teachers and Others Who Follow Their Hearts*, are beloved in the early childhood education field.

Jackie Cooke, the 2007 Oregon State Teacher of the Year, knew she wanted to be a teacher from her first day of first grade. She now has been teaching for twenty-five years, and currently teaches first-graders. She has a special passion for teaching students strong math skills and helping them master technology.

Linda DeMino Duffy teaches kindergarten inclusion classes in San Antonio, Texas, which means she teaches and supports special education students who are mainstreamed into regular classrooms. She was named 2001 Texas State Teacher of the Year and speaks frequently at teacher conferences and workshops. She was drawn to teaching children with special needs after volunteering during her senior year in high school at the Special Olympics.

Dara Feldman taught kindergarten in Maryland and was named a 2005 Disney Teacher Award honoree before leaving the classroom to start her own company, "The Heart of Education." Its mission is to provide strategies for educational professionals, students, and families that encourage the growth of ethical character.

Susie Haas-Kane is a California kindergarten teacher who was inducted into the National Teachers Hall of Fame in 2000. She was named California State Teacher of the Year in 1999, and was a Disney Teacher Award honoree in 1999. She is known nationwide for her Early Literacy Instruction seminars and for her fun, creative, and inspiring classroom ideas.

Randy Heite, a kindergarten teacher in Illinois, was chosen as a Disney Teacher Award honoree in 2003. In addition to his many other creative classroom projects, his annual "kindergarten diner," where his students operate their own restaurant for a day, has become a cherished tradition in his community.

Pauline Jacroux, who teaches first grade in Hawaii, was a Disney Teacher Award honoree in 2003. She says her class garden also teaches her students about biological and cultural diversity, sharing, respect, life cycles, and habitats. Before teaching, she had a career in physical therapy.

Patrice McCrary was named to the 2006 USA Today All-USA Teacher Team, and was Kentucky State Teacher of the Year in 2003. Her class starts the day with a "good morning" in multiple languages, including sign language, and to maintain strong contact with parents, she sends out weekly newsletters and monthly calendars, maintains a website, and sends "news flash" emails.

Stephanie Seay, the 2006 South Carolina Teacher of the Year, teaches kindergarten and presents workshops for teachers on school readiness and assessment. She recalls a little boy named Curtis she met while a student teacher, who reaffirmed her career path. With a grandmother in prison, a mother in drug rehabilitation, and an abusive father, Curtis would often curl open in her lap as they read together. On her final day, he gave her a letter that read: "I love you because you are my teacher."

Patti Teel is the creator of an audio series that teaches children relaxation exercises based in yoga, visualizations, music, and storytelling. A children's music specialist and a special education teacher, she considers her ability to connect with children to be her greatest gift. Her book, *The Floppy Sleep Game Book*, and its audio CD have helped tens of thousands of families across the country by teaching children how to soothe themselves to sleep.

Nancy Weber is a former classroom teacher with over thirty years' experience in the field of education. She is a nationally known professional speaker and educational consultant who has presented over 2,000 seminars and keynote speeches throughout the United States and Canada. She is the coauthor of *Teacher Talk: What It Really Means,* and wrote the lead chapter in the 2003 NAEYC publication *The Power of Guidance.* She lives in Michigan.

OTHER RESOURCES

Teachers' personal bookshelves are often overflowing with great books about kids. Here we've compiled some favorites from several teachers interviewed for this book, as well as a few we consulted for our research that are as useful at home as in the classroom.

The ABCs of Life: Lesson One: The Skills We All Need But Were Never Taught, by Jon Oliver and Michael Ryan (Fireside, 2003)
This book, recommended by Jackie Cooke, teaches important principles necessary for helping children lead happy and productive lives. (And, she notes, it does a good job explaining the three voices she uses in the classroom—animated voice, firm and fair voice, and limit-setting voice.)

Anyway: The Paradoxical Commandments: Finding Personal Meaning in a Crazy World, by Kent M. Keith (Berkley, 2004)
Recommended by Pauline Jacroux, who says: "'Negativity towards life experiences abounds, but do the right thing anyway' is the basis

of these commandments. Last year I started to explain behavior to my first-graders by saying, 'Whatever happened, did you do the right thing?' Believe it or not, this resulted in immediate changes in facial expressions, and stopped the complaining, accusing, crying, or whatever. Children would break into a smile and run off happily laughing."

A Child's Work: The Importance of Fantasy Play, by Vivian Gussin Paley (University of Chicago Press, 2005)
Written by the only kindergarten teacher ever to be recognized with a MacArthur Award "genius grant," this book richly describes children's play. Another of Paley's books, *You Can't Say You Can't Play,* chronicles what happens when the teacher creates a new rule in her kindergarten classroom: "You can't say 'You can't play.'"

Conscious Discipline: Seven Basic Skills for Brain-Smart Classroom Management, by Dr. Becky Bailey (Loving Guidance, 2001)
A choice of two of our teachers, Jackie Cooke and Stephanie Seay, this book is written for the classroom but adaptable for home. Bailey's books more specifically directed to parents include: *Easy to Love, Difficult to Discipline: The Seven Basic Skills for Turning Conflict into Cooperation* and *I Love You Rituals.*

Creative Experiences for Young Children, by Mimi Brodsky Chenfeld (Heinemann, 2002)
The author's contagious joy, creativity, and unbridled sense of fun

are legendary in the early childhood world, and while her books are directed toward teachers, parents will walk away brimming with ideas and a new sense of adventure. Other titles include: *Teaching by Heart* and *Celebrating Young Children and Their Teachers*.

The Floppy Sleep Game Book: A Proven 4-Week Plan to Get Your Child to Sleep and CD, by Patti Teel (Perigee, 2005)
Clearly and comfortingly outlines ways parents can teach their young children relaxation and visualization techniques and help them sleep on their own. You also can download recorded visualizations for children at the author's website, www.timeoutfordreamers.com, or learn more at www.pattiteel.com.

The Hurried Child: Growing Up Too Fast Too Soon, by David Elkind (Perseus, 2001)
A classic parenting guide, this book comes recommended by Nancy Weber, who notes its important message: By blurring the boundaries of what is age-appropriate, we force our kids to grow up too fast. Other titles by the same author include: *Miseducation: Preschoolers at Risk* and *Power of Play: How Spontaneous, Imaginative Activities Lead to Happier, Healthier Children*.

Mr. Rogers Talks with Parents, by Fred Rogers, (Hal Leonard Corporation, 1993)
Recommended by Nancy Weber, who also suggests his other parenting titles, which include: *The Mr. Rogers Parenting Resource Book: Helping*

to Understand and Encourage Your Child and *Many Ways to Say I Love You: Wisdom for Parents and Children from Mister Rogers.*

The New Six Point Plan for Raising Happy, Healthy Children, by John Rosemond (Andrews McMeel, 2006)

Recommended by Pauline Jacroux, who describes this book as "a very practical, commonsense approach to parenting in a world cluttered with so much advice on 'proper' child rearing." The new edition updates the original book (published more than fifteen years ago) and maintains that parents should be their children's leaders rather than their friends.

Off to School: A Parent's View of the Kindergarten Year, by Irene Hannigan (National Association for the Education of Young Children, 1998)

A mom journals her son's journey through kindergarten in this book, recommended by Joan Rice. The author uses her own journal entries, as well as weekly letters home from her son's teacher, to detail her son's growth and development—and her own.

Punished by Rewards: The Trouble with Gold Stars, Incentive Plans, A's, Praise and Other Bribes, by Alfie Kohn (Replica, 2001)

The author shows how rewards undermine efforts to teach students, manage workers, and raise children in this book recommended by Pauline Jacroux, who notes it is "*not* easy reading, but presents another side to our reward-oriented practices of controlling behavior."

Teacher Talk: What It Really Means, by Chick Moorman and Nancy Weber (Personal Power Press, 1989)

Cowritten by one of the teachers we interviewed, Nancy Weber, this book looks at the effect our words have on children. While written with an eye toward things teachers commonly say in the classroom, it's equally applicable to home, and will help parents consider their choice of expressions and questions.